U.S. CAMERA ANNUAL · 1952

EDITED BY TOM MALONEY

Associate Editors

CAMILLE J. PELLETIER • JACK L. TERRACCIANO • WALTER HERDEG

PUBLISHED BY

U.S. CAMERA PUBLISHING CORP. · 420 LEXINGTON AVENUE · NEW YORK CITY

Distributed by Duell, Sloan & Pearce

PRINTED IN U.S.A.

CONTENTS

International Photography

News

CANDID PHOTOGRAPHER   ERIKA

U.S. CAMERA ANNUAL · 1952

A PICTURE book year of unusual variety has passed since U. S. CAMERA 1951 appeared: *Life's* voluminous *Picture History of World War II;* David Duncan's masterly *This Is War,* a photo-narrative; Ansel Adams' *The Print;* another extravaganza by Cecil Beaton; and Condé Nast's (and U. S. Camera's Jonathan Tichenor's) *The Art and Technique of Color Photography,* published by Simon & Schuster, a record of photo color at its most brilliant over three decades, to name leaders. Year by year photo books become increasingly important. And slowly—

still so slowly it takes avid research to recognize—book critics and publishers are accepting the picture book as a normal part of publishing, printing and reading.

Otherwise the last year has been not too rewarding photographically. The Korean war was so well covered through the Inchon landing and our December retreat that later pictures have seemed mainly routine or anti-climactic. General MacArthur's return was handled hectically, as the occasion warranted, and the triumphal reentry gave news photographers a Roman holiday and some fine and friendly shots of the General's reception.

The Kefauver Committee's hearings belong to the ages—through television. The eclipse of the news photographer was not complete, but his best efforts had to play second fiddle to a new medium for seeing. Television brings a new discussion to photography—at present, not by any means a happy one for still-picture work. For the home-viewing screen has become such an extensive part of our living that the process from which it springs cannot continue the uninterrupted march of its own expensive equipment. For many dealers and manufacturers this has been an expensive rather than an expansive year. No one can term the television year a photographically expressive one. The limits of television's expressive ability were keenly highlighted by the Kefauver hearings. The gold is there, but the dross has buried it to a dimensionless depth.

As always, however, there were an extensive number of compensations pictorially. *Life* magazine surpassed its previous self in a series of their photo essays in color that were outstandingly beautiful, and in a few instances breathtaking and wonderful. The color pullout (*see pages 8-17*) of the midnight sun photographed off Norway for 24 hours of the endless day led a grand group of color photo features, such as Jack Breed's *Spring Comes to New England,* Alfred Eisenstaedt's *Jungle Gardens,* Ralph Crane's *Winter in Yellowstone Park* and *The River Thames* by A. William Sumits.

The reproduction of these color stories was so improved through *Life's* engraving process that highest speed presses turned out work of a quality usually expected only in *Vogue* and *Harper's Bazaar.*

The *National Geographic* magazine had issue after issue with outstanding quality—and quantity—of color. Their articles on high speed color camera work by Edgerton, Allen and the Army Air Corps were the year's best. The *Geographic* was using color before most of the best magazine color-users were in existence, yet in 1951 the magazine that has shown no change in format in 62 years continued to be the leader it has always been in color.

The Eastman Kodak Company continued to collect the work of the best American photographers in color. It is regrettable that these pictures are released in random fashion to the public through Eastman's advertising and public relations. Perhaps in the next year they can be collated. Certainly the group work of Adams, Strand, Sheeler, Weston and Atkeson would be a treat to all and a treatment for students of photography.

The black and white highlights start with Philippe Halsman's opening 14 pages. Here is a cross section of the work of one of the most versatile of photographers. The continuing efforts of the Dali-Halsman combination really culminate in the skull of beauty-fantasy. Here is the photo task that calls upon the craftsman to concede to the improbable—and to do the impossible. Halsman's brilliance is so widely used, photographers and readers are likely to forget his importance to photography. This is the genie in the bottle, the magician who does the impossible. Yet there is no hocus *focus* about Halsman. His first gesture will be to show you how simply it was all done.

Eugene Smith's *Spanish Town* photo essay from *Life* is a superb and sombre portrayal. *Life's* photo essays are bound to be variable in quality—sometimes the concept is poor— sometimes the photography just doesn't come off. But more often the concept and photography jell and a fine piece is the result. For this editor the finest of the year was Gene Smith's *Spanish* (*Continued on Page 399*)

3:27 P.M. 4:27 P.M. 5:27 P.M.

WEST

UNFOLD

12:27 P.M.   1:27 P.M.   2:27 P.M.

9:27 A.M.   10:27 A.M.   11:27 A.M.

SOUTH

6:27 P.M.   7:27 P.M.   8:27 P.M.   9:27 P.M.

10:27 P.M.   11:27 P.M.   12:27 A.M.

NORTH

6:27 A.M.   7:27 A.M.   8:27 A.M.

Arctic Sun In Color

Color panorama by Swiss photographers Schulthess and Spühler shows the full sweep of the midnight sun.

(Courtesy Life Magazine)

WRITING in *Du*, the Swiss magazine in whose Christmas issue first appeared this dramatic series of color photos, Emil Schulthess says:

"At first, we had planned to take one large color photo with a wide angle lens which would show the sun at short intervals during the midnight hours. But after talking it over with friends we got new ideas and the thought was born to produce a 24-hour panorama of the sun. We made a rough sketch of our plans on a globe, but because of the bad weather along the northwest coast of Norway, most of the competent scientists we knew did not give us much chance of success. And besides there was the problem of photographing the sun directly without getting disturbing reflections. To solve this problem we attached two crosswires of very thin nylon fishing lines to a wooded frame, and at the intersection of the lines glued a small semi-opaque disc which would obscure the sun. Tests proved that this idea was *(Continued on Page 17)*

2:27 A.M.   3:27 A.M.   4:27 A.M.

a practical one and the desired effect could be accomplished.

"All preparations had to be hurried because we were close to the 21st of June, the date we had set for the start of the experiments, the day when the sun would swing highest above the horizon.

"We flew to Norway, and the meteorological station of Tromsoe helped us to pick the most favorable spot, which was the small island of Hekkingen at the mouth of the Malangeu Fjord. We arrived by steamer at Loekvik on the island, where, with the help of natives we brought our equipment to the top of a hill. It was 11:30 p.m. of June 24 so we had little time to lose, since we wanted to start photographing the series of 24 hourly pictures at 5:27 a.m. on June 25. There was a lot to be done between each hourly photo. Every hour Emile Spühler, who had the responsibility for the photo techniques of this difficult undertaking, and I measured the intensities of light and color as well as the temperatures in sun and shade."

From the family of fishermen, the sole occupants of the island, Schulthess and Spühler had obtained a small fly-tent and a few supplies of milk, fish and sea-gull eggs which were carried up to the top of the mountain from which the photographs were made. The tent is visible in the photo taken at 6:27 a.m. and in the one taken at 2:27 p.m. can be seen one of the small fishing boats of the village returning with its catch. These are the only visible signs of life in the entire panorama.

They started photographing at 5:27 a.m. of June 25. They selected 27 minutes past the hour because they would be able to catch the sun at its highest and lowest points which would be reached at 11:27 a.m. and 11:27 p.m. respectively.

For several hours everything went on schedule, except for a few light clouds which at times almost obscured the sun. Around 1 p.m. thunder clouds began to assemble, and by 3 p.m. the storm broke. The two men hurriedly disassembled their equipment and rushed it into the tent, which they had to hold down because of the strong winds. Fortunately none of the equipment was damaged and in about an hour the storm had subsided but it was too late to take the 11th picture (3:27 p.m.). Rather than break the sequence, the photographers decided to wait until the next day and take up again where they had left off. After spending the night in a fisherman's hut, they returned the following morning, and favored by good weather were able to complete the series.

Schulthess and Spühler then flew back to Zurich where they processed the film. Each print was then cropped with the sun in the center of the panel and a continuous panoramic sequence was achieved.

The photo below shows Schulthess (left) and Spühler with the camera and suspended disc with which they made this experiment.

(These color plates were obtained through the courtesy of Life Magazine. Photos from Black Star.)

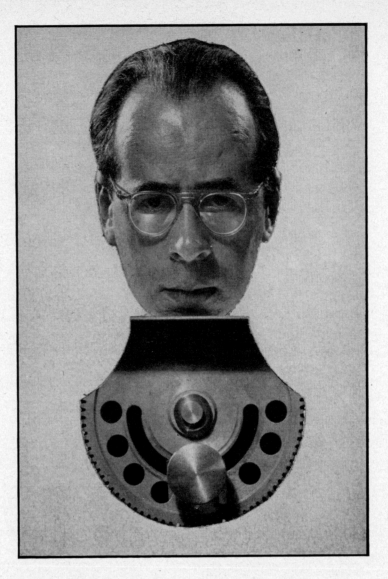

PHILIPPE HALSMAN

THE rarest of all photographers is he who knows and responds to the agony of an editor who has gone through his stable of stars to no avail and finally calls on his Jack-of-all-photo-trades—and tricks—to do the impossible. This fellow has photo genes that neither he nor the editor can place—but the editor knows if those genes can be found anywhere they will be available in his man of last recall.

There is no better practitioner of this lens versatility in America today than a lithe, little Latvian with a facile French name, Philippe Halsman, a series of whose photos appears on pages 18-31.

Halsman has had 50 covers on *Life* (more than any other photographer). Halsman can take the most cockeyed of Salvador Dali's conceptions (*see pages 20-22*) and recreate it in the photo idiom. Halsman treats the female form as though only he (and the Deity) can capture all of its infinite expressions *sans* attire. Halsman can make the sublime hilarious—and could probably make the hilarious sublime if called on to do so—a last resort that some editor will undoubtedly ask for in the near future.

If *Life* wants it á la *Vogue*, Halsman's the man. If *Vogue* wants it á la *Life*, the call goes out for Halsman. And if someone wants something just for the fun of it—with a world of fun in it—it's Halsman. (*Continued on Page 386*)

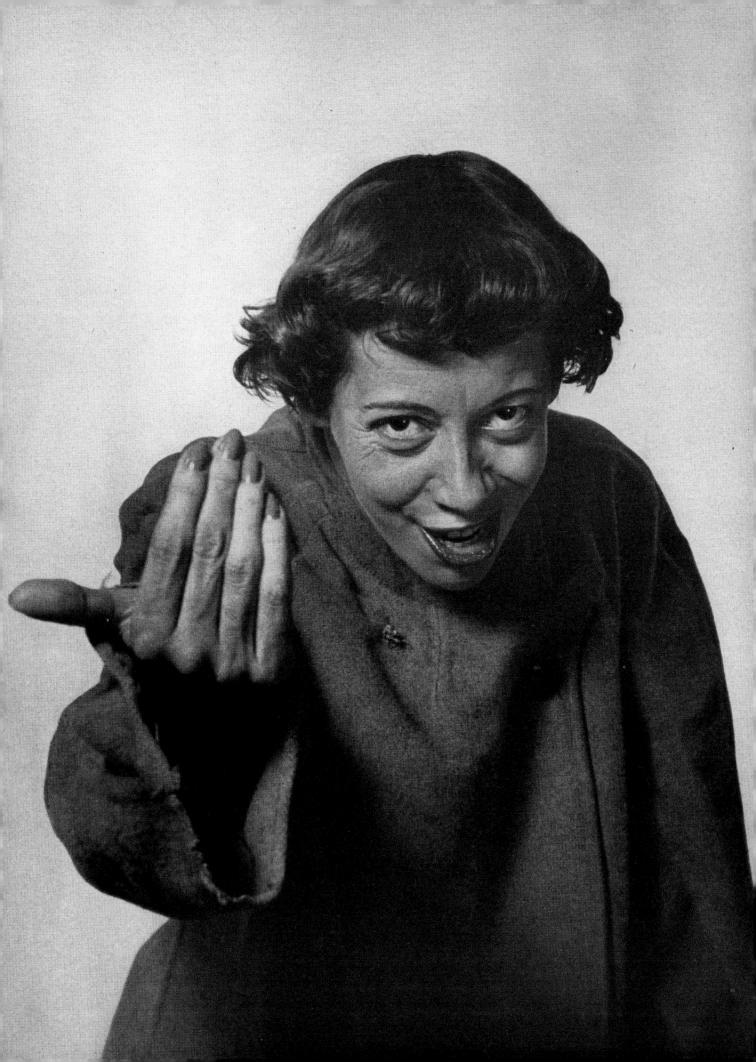

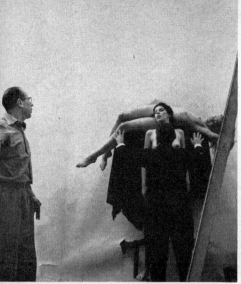

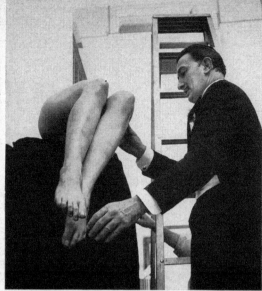

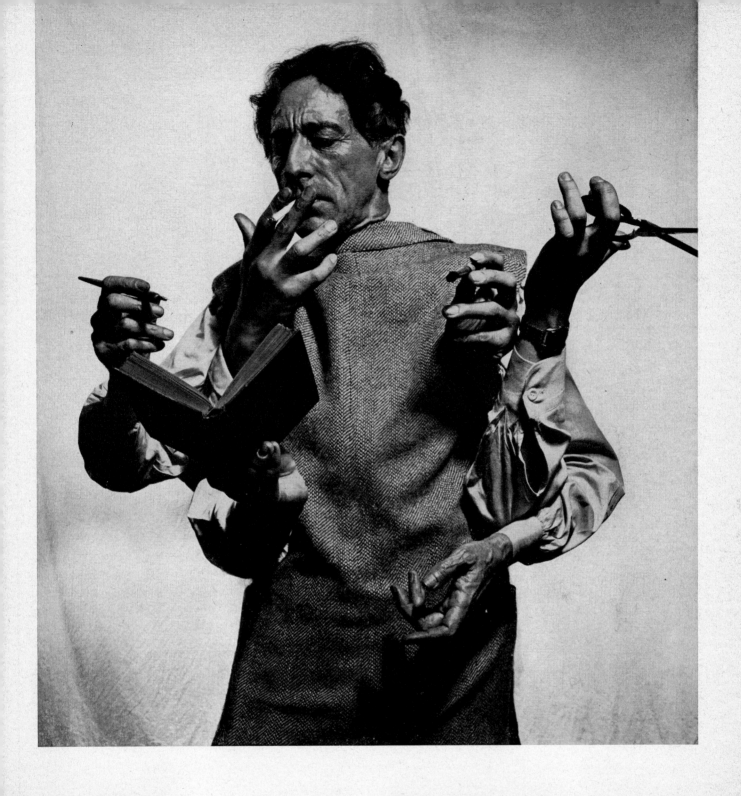
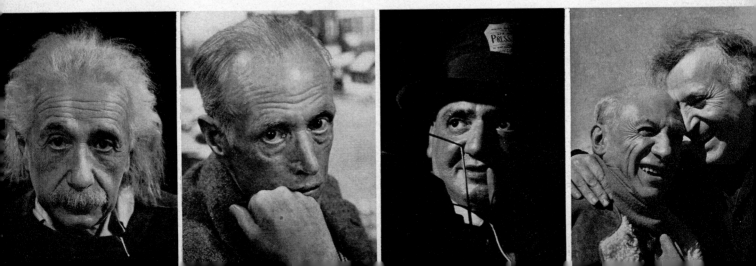

ARTHUR SIEGEL   PLANT 1950

ANTHONY J. CUTRONEO   NUDE

ANTHONY CANEDO

PROFILE (PAGE 34)

By using a single spotlight held high and to the extreme right of the subject, Canedo was able to achieve the unusual inter-play of tones and textures pictured on the left. Presently enrolled as an English major at the University of Washington, Canedo has been taking pictures for six years. Although he has done medical photography for the University, his present interests lie in the direction of experimental lighting and darkroom techniques. The profile study was made with a 3¼x4¼ view camera equipped with a 10″ Goerz Dagor lens, with exposure on Super-XX film.

PAUL WELLER

MR. ROBSJOHN-GIBBINGS (PAGE 36)

A distinguished painter and teacher of fine arts, Paul Weller began his photographic career after serving in the U. S. Army during World War II. His study of Robsjohn-Gibbings, one of the world's leading decorators and designers of furniture, was made for *Flair* magazine. Natural light was used, with the exposure made at 1/10th of a second at f/5.6 on a Rolleiflex camera and Super-XX film. The influence of Weller's fine arts training on his photographic treatments can be seen in the graceful lines and composition of the picture on *page 36*. Honored with a one-man show at the Brooklyn Museum of Art, Weller devotes most of his time to advertising and magazine photography.

LEONARD McCOMBE

W. SOMERSET MAUGHAM

A 27-year-old English photographer born on the remote Isle of Man, Leonard McCombe first gained international prominence for his photographs of East German refugees at the end of World War II. During the war he had covered assignments for the English pictorial magazine *Picture Post* as well as work for the British Ministry of Information. In 1946 McCombe came to the United States to work for *Life* Magazine and has been doing assignments for them ever since.

While on a *Life* assignment to document candid moments during the recent visit of W. Somerset Maugham, McCombe spent several days photographing the noted British writer as he shopped, walked the streets, and worked or relaxed in his hotel room. In the photo at right, he caught Maugham as he waited in vain for a taxi on Madison Ave. during the rush-hour in New York. Using a Contax, McCombe exposed at 1/125th of a second with aperture set at f/4, on Super-XX.

PAUL WELLER   ROBSJOHN-GIBBINGS

F. W. GRUNZWEIG   U.N. WINDOW WASHER

F. W. GRUNZWEIG

U.N. WINDOW WASHER (PAGE 37)

"I am an International Civil Servant," writes F. W. Grunzweig, now serving with the U.N. Secretariat. "For some time, I studied the window washers in a variety of positions, attempting to visualize the effect captured here." Taking the picture at noon on an exceptionally bright and windy day, Grunzweig used a Standard Rolleiflex with a Tessar f/3.8 lens, exposing at 1/100th of a second, at an aperture of f/16, using a K-2 yellow filter.

LEONARD McCOMBE

ROPING A MOUNT (PAGES 40-41)

In this photograph Leonard McCombe has caught the thundering excitement of the corral as a cowpuncher ropes his mount for the day's work in the round-up. This is one from a series done on assignment for *Life* to document the modern cowboy working on a Texas ranch. The story has recently been published in book form, titled "The Cowboy", and the reportage also won for McCombe the award of "Photographer of the Year" from the University of Missouri School of Journalism and the Encyclopaedia Britannica. McCombe used a Contax, shooting at 1/250th of a second with an aperture of f/8.

GEORGE A. SMALLSREED, JR.

LIGHTS OUT

In order to freeze the action of the two fighters pictured on the right, George Smallsreed, Jr., of the *Columbus Dispatch,* used 2 1,000-watt SR Strobe units, divided into 8 individual lighting units. The units were evenly suspended over the ring area, so as to provide full illumination over the entire field of action. Stopping his f/4.5 Optar lens down to f/32, with the SR unit giving off a light flash of approximately 1/1000th of a second, Smallsreed used a Pacemaker Speed Graphic and Kodak Super-XX film. Joining the *Dispatch* in 1946, after serving five years in the U. S. Navy, Smallsreed was placed in charge of all the staff photographers in July of 1949.

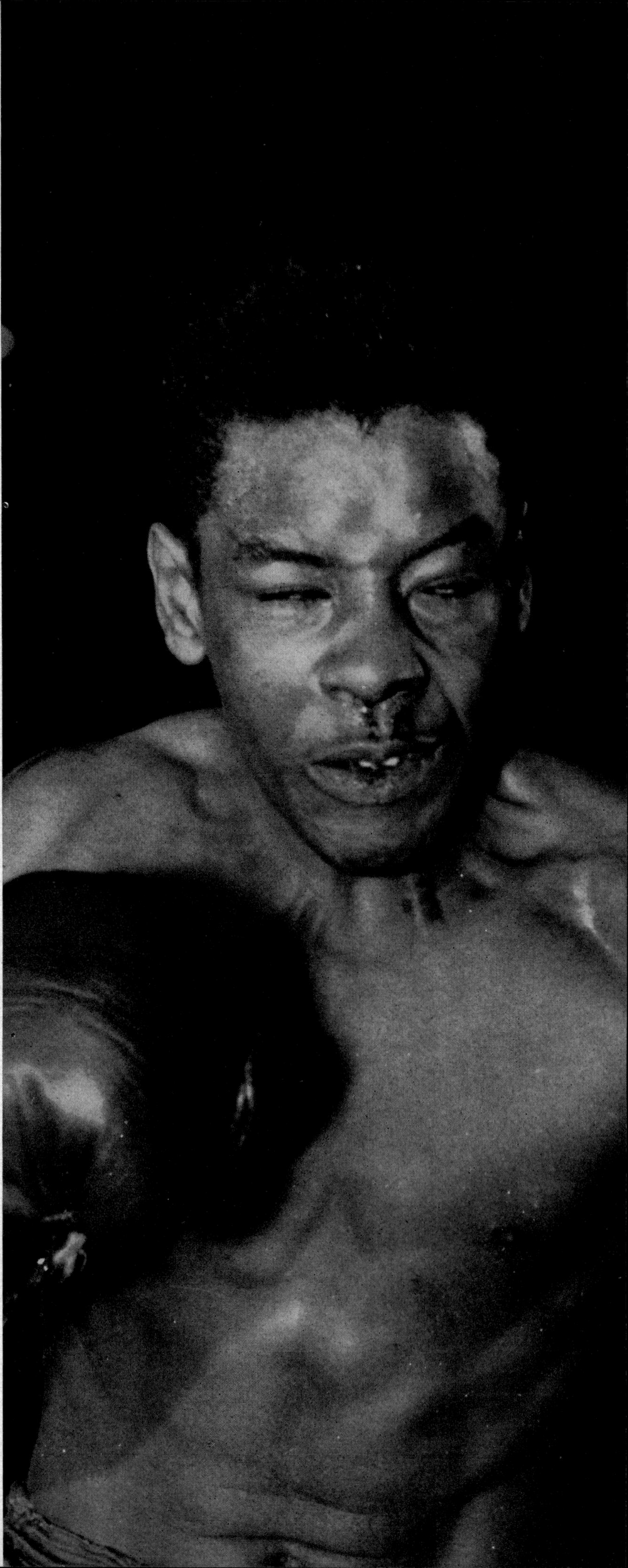

FERENC BERKO

Ferenc Berko's keen and searching interest in unusual photographic approaches is attested to by the wide variety of his work, typical of which, are the two pictures above and to the right. The nude is one of a series of experiments that Berko has made with solarized techniques. By making copy negatives from old prints, using extreme high contrast film, he is able to eliminate the half-tone quality. After the copy negative is made, Berko makes a contact print; repeating the process with the same negative until he achieves the desired effect. In this case the original negative was made with a Leica, then the negative for solarization was made with a 4 x 5 studio view camera.

Born in Hungary, Berko has studied and worked in studios throughout Europe and the East, and is now working in Aspen, Colorado. The poppy stalks on the right were photographed after a winter storm with an Automatic Rolleiflex, at an aperture of f/3.5, with a shutter speed of 1/250th of a second, without a filter on Plus-X film.

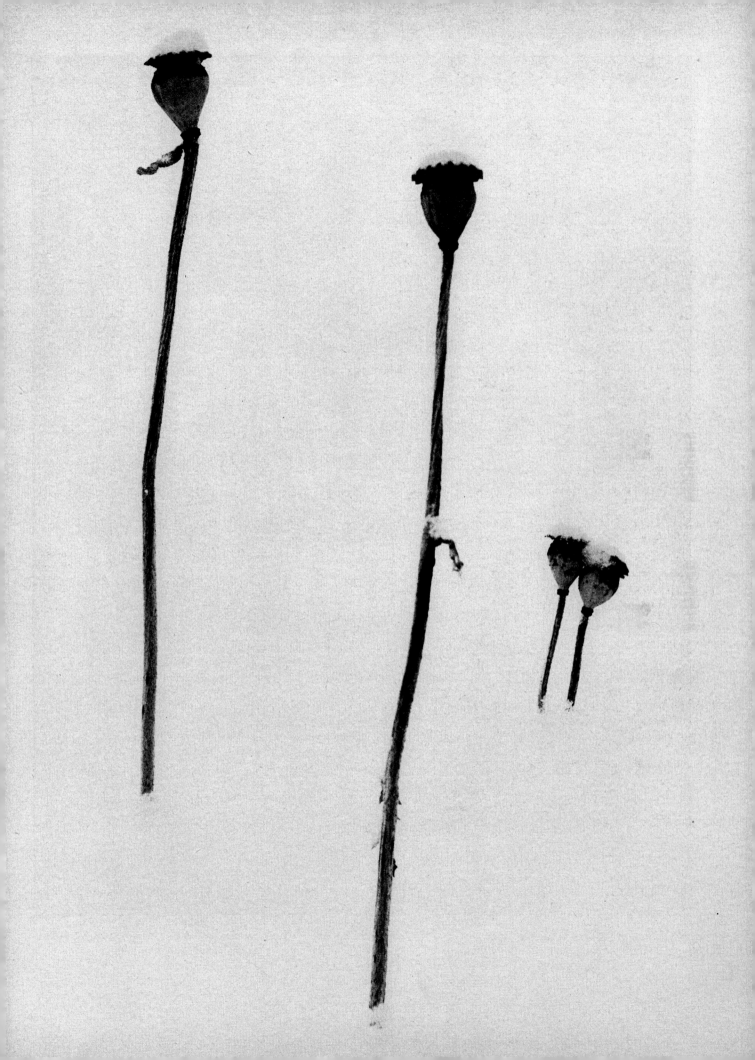

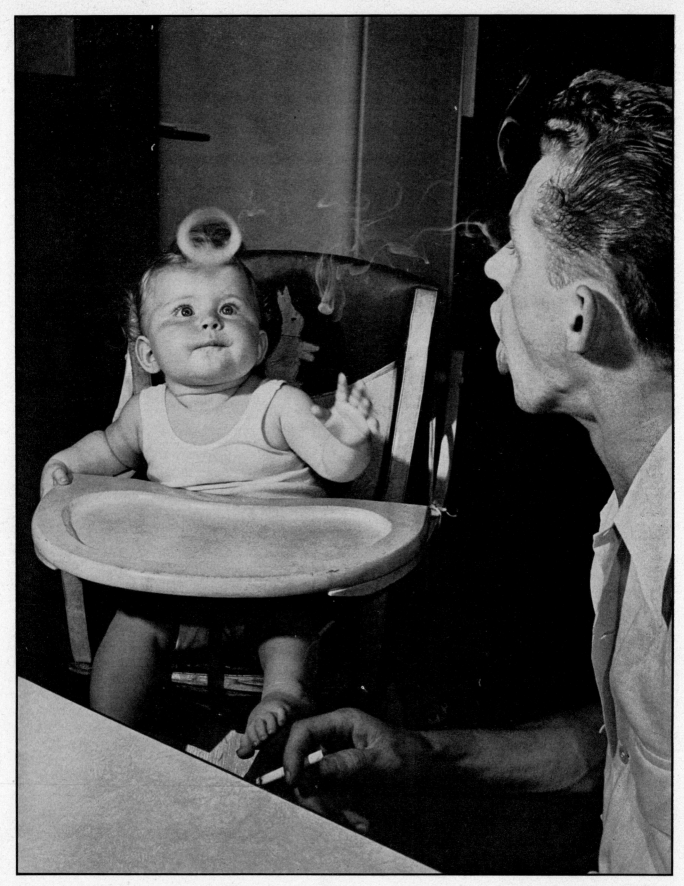

JOSEPH WASILAUSKAS   SMOKE RINGS

JOSEPH WASILAUSKAS

SMOKE RINGS

This "self portrait" at the left, taken with an extra long cable release, won for Joseph Wasilauskas of Waterbury, Conn. the Grand Prize of $1,000 and the $500 First Prize in the Class B section of the National Newspaper Snapshot contest. An avid amateur photographer, Wasilauskas was the winner in the local competition sponsored by the *Waterbury Sunday Republican* in Connecticut.

RAY ELSTEAD

BLURRED ACTION

Ray Elstead's amusing shot of a harried young man won an honor award in the Non-Professional Action division of the 1950 Graflex Photography Contest. Using a relatively slow shutter speed enabled the photographer to convey a feeling of high-speed action. Elstead, a native Californian, used a 4 x 5 Pacemaker Speed Graphic, exposing with natural light on Super-XX film to get the desired effect.

BRETT WESTON

Brett Weston, son of Edward Weston, is heir to a distinguished photographic tradition. A listing of places and publications using photographs by Edward Weston would make a veritable roll-call of many of the leading museums and publications in the Western World. Starting his own career at the age of 13, Brett Weston sold his first picture two years later.

His technique, the subject matter that is of prime importance to him, shows the strong influence of his father's early guidance. Unlike many contemporary photographers, Weston refuses to "make" photographs in the darkroom by artful developing, enlarging and retouching techniques. Instead, he uses extreme care in setting up his picture, composing

WALT WIGGINS

NEW MEXICO LANDSCAPES (PAGE 48)

After service with the Signal Corps during the war, Wiggins returned to New Mexico to do photo-journalistic work in the Southwest. His two landscapes on *page* 48 were taken

with a Rolleiflex and Super-XX film. For the valley photo he exposed for 1/100th of a second at f/11, while the road shot was made in 1/100th of a second at f/8.

directly on a ground glass, making contact prints from the original negative. The pictures above appear in "Special Editions 1951", a collection of his personalized photographs. "Storm over Barns" was made while Weston was in Virginia on a *Guggenheim* fellowship. It was taken with an 8 x 10 Ansco Commercial View camera with a 19″ Goerz Dagor lens. The remarkable depth of field was made possible by Weston stopping down the lens to an aperture of f/45 exposing for ½ a second on Isopan film. For the picture titled "Surf", Weston mounted a 21″ Kodak process lens on an 8 x 10 view camera. He made an exposure of 1/50th of a second with an aperture of f/22 on Isopan fine grain film.

LEON LEVINSTEIN

OLD LADY (PAGE 49)

"I've been taking photographs every Saturday, Sunday and holidays for the past 3½ years," writes Levinstein. "I always attempt to project to the viewer of my photographs my feelings about persons or places." The picture on *page 49* was taken on the lower East Side of New York City, with a Rolleiflex at 1/50th of a second on Super-XX at f/11.

ANDRE DE DIENES   BEACH NUDES

After studying art and travelling on the continent, De Dienes settled in Paris, where he undertook a two-year apprenticeship in photography. In 1938 he came to America, where his name has become synonymous with top caliber fashion and advertising photography. He has also developed remarkable techniques for portraying the nude. Using natural light where possible, De Dienes stresses spontaneity in the human form, as shown in the pictures above and to the right. Both models were photographed with a minimum amount of posing, in an effort to capture a feeling of freedom. A Rolleiflex equipped with a Tessar f/3.5 lens was used, with exposures of 1/100th of a second on Panchromatic film.

DON BRIGGS   FIGURE STUDIES (PAGE 52)

"This figure," writes Briggs, "is a typical example of the techniques we are developing in Kaminski's creative photography group. The purpose of these techniques is to enable the photographer to completely control the final result so that he may express his feelings about a subject rather than record the subject itself. This creative approach makes photography a contemporary medium instead of a tired recording device from the last century." Briggs made the enlargements on Kodalitht, printing two of the negatives from positive proofs and the third from a negative so as to produce white lines against a middle grey. A Rolleiflex was used, at 1/25th of a second on Kodak Plus-X film with normal studio lighting.

EDWARD LETTAU   NUDES

A specialist in child photography, Lettau constantly experiments with lighting techniques in an effort to widen the scope of his commercial efforts. His studies of the nude form at the right were made with three speedlight units and a 4x5 Super D Graflex. All three exposures were made at an aperture of f/32 with the speedlights giving off a light flash approximately 1/1000th of a second in duration. The unusual rendition of tones and textures resulted from Lettau's extensive arrangement and adjusting of the speedlight units.

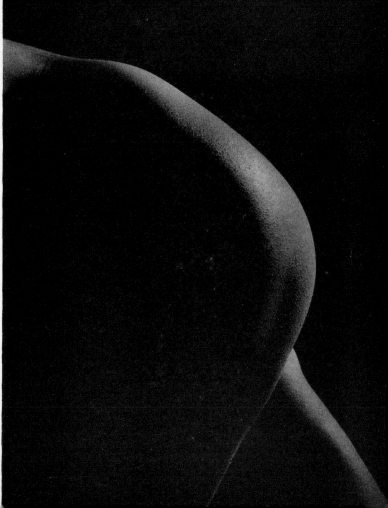

ANSEL ADAMS

THE FISHING CONE (PAGES 56-57)

Ansel Adams was born in San Francisco in 1902, and started his distinguished photographic career in 1927. He lives in the Yosemite Valley, and has photographed that region for many years throughout the four seasons and their varying moods. The picture on *pages 56-57* courtesy of the United States Department of the Interior, is typical of the majestic sweep, dignity, grandeur, and above all the technical excellence of his work. Twice the recipient of a *Guggenheim Fellowship,* he has had his documentative photographs exhibited and published in many countries, so that today, Adams has no peer as a recorder and pictorial interpreter of America's National Parks. *The Fishing Cone* was photographed in Yellowstone National Park in Wyoming. The sand in the foreground of the picture was only a few feet from the lens, but by means of a tilting camera back, Adams was able to convey a feeling of extreme depth and vastness. He used an 8x10 studio Ansco Commercial View camera, with a 12½" Cooke Anastigmat lens. The exposure was made on Ansco Isopan film, at a shutter speed of 1/10th of a second at an aperture of f/45.

REGINALD McGOVERN

"WHOOM!"

Outstanding news photographs catch for posterity those all-too-brief moments that make history: fleeting expressions, sudden flare-ups, off-guard poses of celebrities; split-second events that must be caught at the right instant or forever lost. To the long and distinguished list of news pictures taken at the right instant, can be added this remarkable on-the-spot photograph by Reginald McGovern. All the drama of fire-fighting; the very impact and resulting danger of a cataclysmic chemical explosion are captured here by an alert witness.

In order to cover the large area before him, McGovern had to open his aperture to f/4.5, as he was using a small No. 5 flash bulb. Working with a Speed Graphic, he shot at 1/200th of a second on Super Panchro Press film with an Ektar 5-inch coated lens.

Although he is only 31 years old, McGovern, now a staff photographer on the Redwood City *Tribune* of California, has been taking pictures for 14 years. Included in his background are periods with a commercial studio and free-lance assignments on the West Coast.

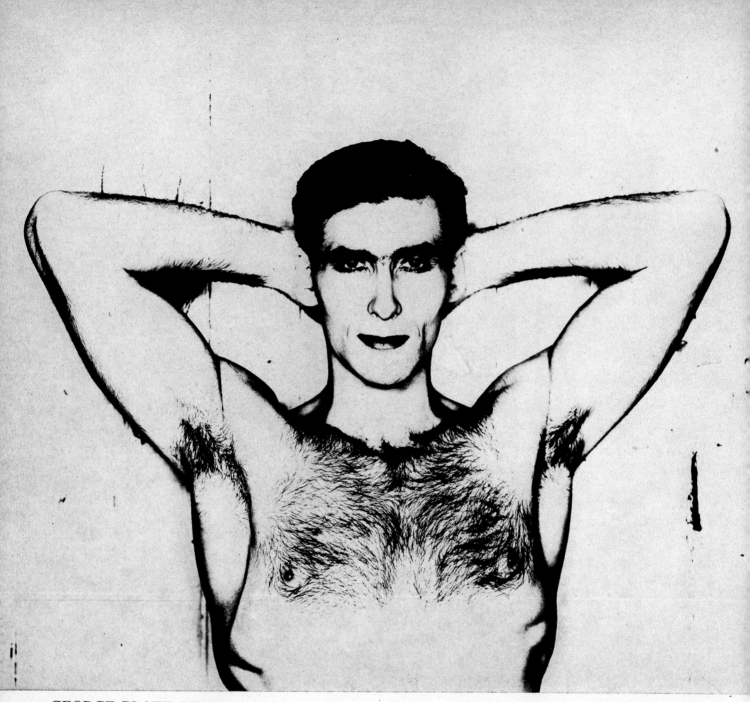

GEORGE PLATT LYNES

IGOR YOUSKEVITCH

A distinguished portrait and fashion photographer, George Platt Lynes has had studios in Paris, New York and Los Angeles. His study of Youskevitch, premier danseur of the

Ballet Theatre, was made with a Deardoff 8 x 10 studio view camera. A Goerz Dagor 12-inch lens was used, with studio lighting and exposure on Commercial Ortho film.

FRITZ NEUGASS

TRIANGLE

"The sailor just started to take his picture when I grabbed my camera, fell to the ground and shot immediately, without even taking time to focus," explains Fritz Neugass, American editor of the Swiss *Camera* magazine. Neugass is an accomplished writer, having had picture-stories published in

Life, Flair, Coronet, Seventeen, and in outstanding European publications. For this picture, he used a Leica camera, an f/3.5 wide-angle lens, Plus-X film, an aperture of f/9, and a shutter speed of 1/100th of a second. Neugass took the photograph near the Lincoln Memorial in Washington, D.C.

WAYNE BULLOCK

"I am a professional photographer who takes every spare moment from commercial work to experiment with new techniques," writes Wayne Bullock. Recently I have received a United States Patent Right on a method of controlling line effect in black and white and color solarization." Bullock

has also been honored with one man shows at the Los Angeles Exposition Park Museum, the Santa Barbara Museum and the Museum of Modern Art in San Francisco. The typewriter was photographed with an Ansco 8x10 View camera. Using Isopan film, Bullock made a time exposure at f/4.5.

LEON LEVINSTEIN

An advertising layout artist, Levinstein's photographic approach can rightfully be called 'a slice of life', for his work always mirrors the reality of his subject matter. Paying little heed to technical considerations, other than what is necessary and fundamental, Levinstein is always striving to "make

photographs simple, direct and true to the medium itself." The study on the right was made with an Automatic Rolleiflex and a Zeiss Tessar f/3.5 lens. Exposing at 1/50th of a second, at an aperture of f/11, Levinstein used Super-XX shooting in late afternoon on New York's lower East Side.

HAROLD E. FOSS

PERSPECTIVE

Since 1939, except for four years with the Air Force in the South Pacific, Harold Foss has been a staff photographer for the U.S. Bureau of Reclamation, at Ephrata, Washington. This photograph was taken while on a routine assignment for the Bureau in the Columbia Basin Irrigation Project. "This square structure," writes Foss, "is called a 'concrete chute' and is used to convey water at high velocities to a lower level from one of the huge canals of the irrigation system. The straight lines and deep shadow made it a 'natural' for a shot of this kind." Infra-red film and an A filter were used to produce the strong contrast. The camera was a Pacemaker Speed Graphic, Kodak Ektar lens, with aperture set at f/16 and a shutter speed of 1/10th of a second.

62

ROBERT FRANK

INDIANS OF PERU

Although most of his work is in the field of fashion photography, Robert Frank made this dramatic portrait study of a Peruvian family while on a recent trip to that country. It shows them cooking and eating the noon-day meal in front of the stone hut in which they live. Because the houses are built without chimneys all of the cooking must be done out of doors. The woman with the straw hat in the foreground is carrying her baby in a shawl on her back. Frank made the photograph with a Leica near the village of Cuzco, Peru, which is at an elevation of about 3500 meters.

Robert Frank came to the United States from Switzerland for the first time in 1947, and, except for one year which he spent photographing in Paris, has been free-lancing in New York City, doing fashion assignments for several national magazines. His work has also been exhibited at the *Museum of Modern Art*.

SANFORD H. ROTH   **PARISIAN CHILD**

While browsing through the book shops on the Rue de Seine in Paris one morning, Roth happened to spot this little child carrying a briefcase and made the photograph with a Contax, Sonnar 50cm lens. He made an exposure of 1/25th of a second with aperture set at f/8. The print was recently acquired by the *Museum of Modern Art* in New York.

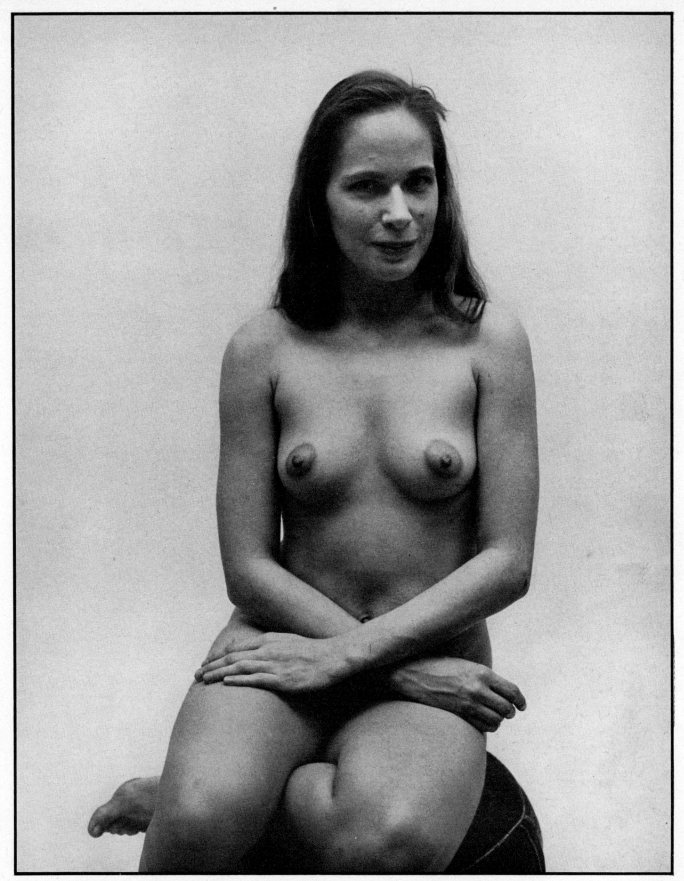

DAVID LINTON

"As a magazine photographer," writes David Linton, "I am primarily interested in people and the events that are important to them. To me the emphasis should always be on what a picture has to say; not how it was made." Linton used a Rolleiflex exposing at 1/10th of a second at f/5.6 with floods reflected from the floor and ceiling.

WALTER FARYNK

PATTERNS (PAGE 70)

As photographer for General Motors, Farynk's assignments run the gamut from microscopic studies of machine parts to mural photographs of tanks and planes. His versatility is demonstrated by the series of pictures on page 70 entitled "The Seeing Eye." Using a 4x5 View camera with a series of interchangeable Ektar lenses, Farynk attempts to record objects and capture moods too often overlooked by photographers working on strict assignments with little spare time for experimentation.

J. R. FLYNN

RHESUS MONKEY (PAGE 71)

A teacher of languages, Flynn is a "confirmed amateur," writing that he prefers to take pictures of everything and anything that interests him. Paying little heed to specialized techniques, Flynn, a native of Utah, has developed a flexibility that is often beyond the ken of a photographer working on strict assignments. A Retina II miniature camera was used, at an aperture of f/5.6, with Flynn exposing at 1/100th of a second on Plus-X film to get the Rhesus monkey on page 71. The subject is an experimental animal at a neurological research center.

ROGER COSTER

WEDDING IN MONTMARTRE

One of the most prolific of all magazine photographers, Coster was born and raised in France. After studying photography in Paris he joined *Pathe,* the French motion picture company as a still photographer. Following the collapse of France's Armies and his subsequent military discharge, Coster came to America in 1941. Prior to entering the U.S. Air Force, he was a staff photographer for *Condé Nast* publications. At present, he is on the staff of *Holiday* magazine. For the picture on the left, he used a Rolleiflex, exposing at 1/100th of a second on Super-XX film.

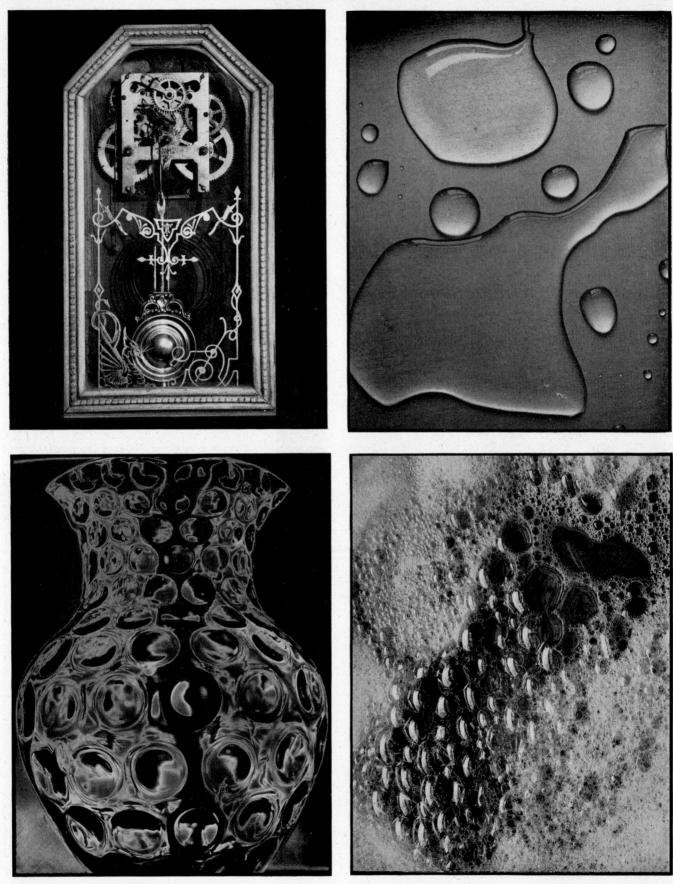

WALTER FARYNK

PATTERNS

J. R. FLYNN

RHESUS MONKEY

BERNIE CLEFF

MARKET PLACE

"I first became interested in photography while a student of design at the School of Art of the Philadelphia Museum," writes Bernie Cleff. Abandoning design for a photographic career, Cleff still studies painting and drawing, for he maintains that "a background in these particular phases of art helps me see things in a more selective manner." Most of Cleff's work lies in the realm of the picture-story since he "prefers this approach, believing that a photographer's job is to show our moods, our social systems; to express what we feel is ugly and what is beautiful." While doing an assignment on the market places in Philadelphia, Cleff saw what to him were two typical women shoppers. "They seemed to personify," he writes, "the feeling, the pleasure that goes with bargaining and browsing in market places." A Rolleiflex with a Xenar f/3.5 lens was used for this photograph.

74

This magnificent photograph is believed to be the only one ever taken showing the twin glaciers of Mt. McKinley—as a rule only the two famed peaks project above the thick bank of clouds that usually hide the glaciers from aerial view. The exposure was made from a single engine plane that circled the periphery of Mt. McKinley at 6,000 feet above sea-level. Using a reinforced Crown Graphic equipped with an Ilex lens, Sweet took the picture on Super Panchro-Press Type-B film, at an aperture of f/16, with a shutter speed of 1/200th of a second. In order to cut through the hazy atmosphere, a K-2 filter was used. The picture is one of a series of over 4,000 black-and-white photographs that Sweet made during a six-month stay in Alaska photographing its scenic beauty.

Considered to be one of America's most prolific magazine cover photographers, Sweet averages about 100 covers a year most of which portray outdoor scenes. His assignments from publications, advertising agencies and top national clients testify to his photographic abilities. His first commercial recognition came while he was an officer in the U. S. Army Signal Corps. One of his 'staged' battle illustrations appeared on the cover of *Newsweek* magazine marking the starting point of an Army photographic career that saw him sell over 100 color shots made while on weekend passes. After his discharge from the Army, Sweet joined the staff of *Newsweek* as a cover photographer, but later left to concentrate on free-lance work in editorial and advertising fields.

TY COTTA

Shooting through an open church door, Ty Cotta stopped his Rolleiflex all the way down to f/22 to get this interesting photograph of deep contrasts and design. An exposure of 1/25th of a second was made on Super XX film. During the war Cotta served as a Signal Corps photographer with the Army and also covered the Nurnberg War Crime Trials.

DAVID STANLEY

GULL ISLAND LIGHT (PAGE 77)

David Stanley's photograph on *page 77* is part of series that were made by a group of photographers who traveled to Mohawk Island, in Lake Erie, in an effort to cover, as comprehensively as possibly, all aspects of the breeding and nesting cycle of gulls and terns.

An instructor and writer of photography, Stanley does advertising and magazine work from his home in Phoenix, Arizona.

"This shot *(page 77)*," writes Stanley, was made to illustrate the effect of sunlight on the leading edges of the wings as well as the formation of the birds in flight. Two people are required to make this type of picture since the gulls rarely leave their nests during the breeding cycle. One person has to run into the nesting area, scattering the birds into flight, in such a way as to divert them towards the preset picture area." Stanley used a Kodak Medalist II and exposed for 1/400th of a second at f/8 on Super XX film.

ROBERT CHAPMAN

STOCK FARM

A real estate broker by profession, Chapman developed a keen interest in photography during World War II, when, as an officer in the Transportation Corps, he kept an extensive documentary record of his service travels in Hawaii, Italy, North Africa and at military bases throughout the United States. After the war, he attended evening courses in photography at the Rochester Institute of Technology. Recognition of his work came early in 1950, when he won First Prize in the Baby Class of the National Newspaper Snapshot Contest. Of late, he has exhibited both color and black-and-white photographs at the 15th annual Rochester International Salon of Photography. For the pictorial study on the right, Chapman used a Korona View camera, an Ilex 4.5 lens, exposing on Super Pan Type B film at 1/50th of a second at f/32.

LEO LEE   NUDE

LOU BERNSTEIN   RANDY KYLE

LOU BERNSTEIN

RANDY KYLE (PAGE 80)

Classifying himself as a "Sunday photographer", Lou Bernstein spends the rest of the week as a salesman in one of New York's largest camera stores. Primarily interested in documentary realism, Bernstein likes to roam the streets of the city or around the countryside in search of photographs which can be taken without benefit of artificial poses or tricky lighting. His excellent portrait of the late Randy Kyle *(page 80)*, former mayor and local guide of Hurleyville, N.Y. was taken with a Rolleiflex at 1/100th of a second on Super-XX film at an aperture of f/11.

LEO LEE

NUDE (PAGE 81)

A fashion and still-life photographer, Leo Lee took this interesting photograph *(page 81)* of a nude by focusing through the converging flats of a half-completed motion picture set. The picture was made with a Rolleiflex on Super-XX film. At present, Lee is working on a photographic book, depicting people at work in various professions.

LOUIS SCHLIVEK

TRAFFIC NIGHTMARE

While doing a series of photographs aimed at catching the emotional impact of traffic jams in New York City, Louis Schlivek took his cue for this photograph from a cabdriver who said, "After a day pushing a hack around in this traffic, I see double." Schlivek purposely double-exposed his Rolleiflex, making one exposure with the cars standing still, and one just as the cars started to move. The camera was also slightly moved to double up the signs in the background. Both pictures were taken in 1/100th of a second at f/11 on Super-XX film.

Schlivek was a sociology student and Phi Betta Kappa at Dartmouth where he first became interested in photography. During the war, he was a script writer, editor and production supervisor with a Signal Corps motion picture unit in the Pacific. After the war he continued in motion picture work, but with his wife, took up still photography. Late in 1947 he began to do picture assignments for the N.Y. *Times Magazine,* and most of his work since then has been done for them.

PETER BASCH

NUDE (PAGE 84)

The novel treatment given this photograph is the result of a series of experiments made by Basch in the control of form, mood and movement, and their relationships to space, composition and balance. Born in Berlin, Peter Basch received his preliminary training in Paris. After his arrival in America, he operated studios in Hollywood and New York. He maintains that "passion motivates the truly creative artist, that the photographer must abandon textbooks and rely on his head and heart instead of filterguides and exposure meters." Using studio light, Basch made this picture with an Automatic Rolleiflex with a f/3.5 Xenar lens.

RICHARD C. SHACKLETT

"STRIKE" (PAGE 85)

"This picture," writes Shacklett, "represents two anxious days of waiting in a fish hatchery. A 5 x 7 Speed Graphic with a 8½" lens, was mounted on a heavy tripod, then placed in an artificial stream so that the camera lens was at near water-level. A fly was suspended above the water, with the lens focused so that any trout lunging for the bait would be within lens range. The trout were apparently frightened by the tripod legs, for they made no attempt to reach the fly. After two days, they weakened, making innumerable lunges for the bait. I made 50 exposures, hoping that the depth of field of my lens, at an aperture of f/4.5, with the camera bellows fully extended, would be great enough to cover the desired field of view in proper focus."

RAY ATKESON

LANDSCAPES (PAGES 86-89)

In 1946 Ray Atkeson abandoned what to him was the strict ritual of commercial studio photography and literally "took off" to the hills, in a long-postponed effort to record the many beauties of the Far West. He photographed the deer *(left)* in the Garibaldi Provincial Park in British Columbia after the first Autumn snow.

While travelling through the Klamath Valley in Oregon, Atkeson noticed the strange atmosphere that was created by the early morning winter vapors *(pages 88-89)*. Here, as with his picture of the deer, Atkeson used a Speed Graphic, shooting at 1/100th of a second at f/16 with a K2 filter to pierce the haze.

HERBERT SCHARFMAN, INP

HOMESTRETCH (PAGE 92)

A specialist in sport news photography, Herbert Scharfman joined *International News Photos* as a motorcycle messenger in 1931. His first assignment as a full-fledged news photographer came ten years later, when he was sent to the New Jersey shore to record the dramatic sinking of small craft during a hurricane. Since that date Scharfman has mastered the use of what is known in the trade as a "Big Bertha" camera; in reality a 5x7 Graflex equipped with a reinforced mount that holds a 40″ telephoto lens. With this lens, Scharfman is able to take long-distance shots; shots far beyond the focal lengths of standard press cameras. The horses, pictured on page 92, were caught as they rounded the last turn heading into the homestrech. Scharfman's keen sense of timing caught the strained facial expressions of the jockeys as they maneuvered their mounts towards the finish line. A shutter speed of 1/1000th of a second at an aperture of f/11 froze the action, with Scharfman using Panchromatic High-Speed film.

EDWARD WESTON

BOULDER DAM

One of the world's best known photographic documentarians, Edward Weston's work bears witness to the philosophy of art that states 'simplicity is beauty'. In an introduction to one of his photographic portfolios Weston wrote, "I do not know any rules of composition nor do I recognize any boundaries to subject matter. Subject matter is everywhere. . . . Whatever it is, its inherent qualities supply the rules of composition for that particular subject within the scope of the medium. I am not a technician and have no interest in technique for its own sake. If my technique is adequate to present my seeing, I need nothing more." His taste for uncluttered simplicity is evident not only in the photograph at the left, but in his darkroom and picture-taking techniques. His darkroom has no enlarger, for he makes direct contact prints from 8x10 negatives. He never crops a negative; instead he composes the final print on the ground glass of his camera. To commemorate the 50th anniversary of his distinguished career, a special personalized portfolio containing a selection of his finest work will be published this Fall. For the picture of the Boulder Dam, Weston used an 8 x 10 camera with a convertible Turner-Reich lens and Ansco Isopan fine grain film.

HERB SCHARFMAN, INP   HOME STRETCH

MAX YAVNO   BOY AT WINDOW

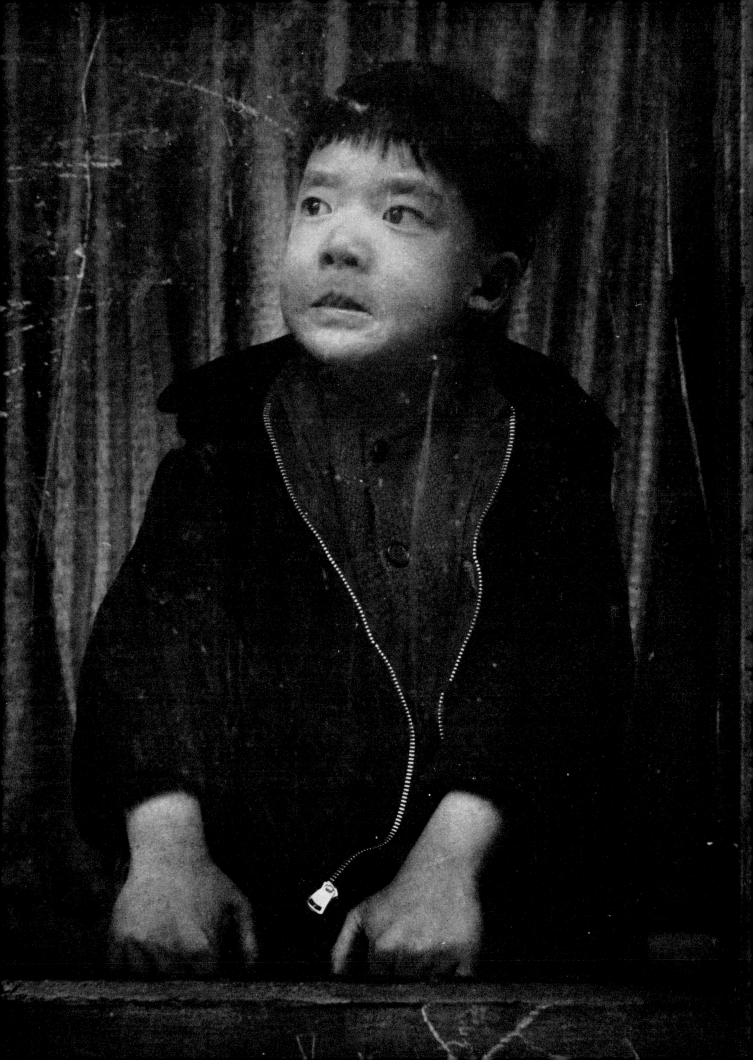

MAX YAVNO

As a sensitive and creative interpreter of the contemporary scene, Max Yavno has few peers. The somewhat mystical, yet honest effect of his work can be illustrated by two of his photographs, the portrait of a boy on *page 93* and the courtyard scene above. Combining documentative approach with an eye for aesthetic visualization, Yavno's

photographs have been exhibited in salons and published throughout the world. The portrait appears in his latest work, *"The San Francisco Book."* It was taken with a 2¼ x 2¼ reflex at 1/25th of a second at f/3.5 on Panchromatic film. A 4 x 5 studio view camera was used in the picture above, with Yavno exposing at 1/5th of a second at f/22.

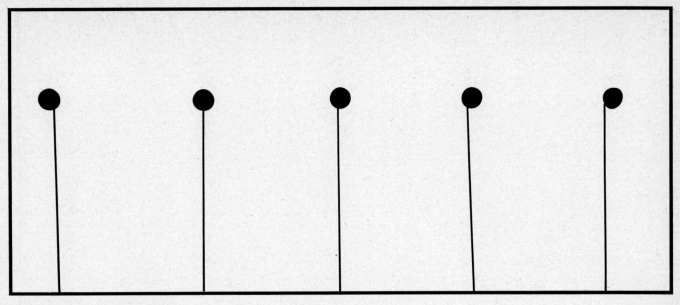

KERMIT E. JOHNSON

Johnson, who is currently with General Motors' photographic department, made these delicate studies in design using a Rolleiflex for the study (*above*) with an exposure of 1/50th of a second at f/11, and a Speed Graphic for the fence in the snow (*below*) making a one second exposure with aperture at f/32. Kodak Super-XX film was used in both cases.

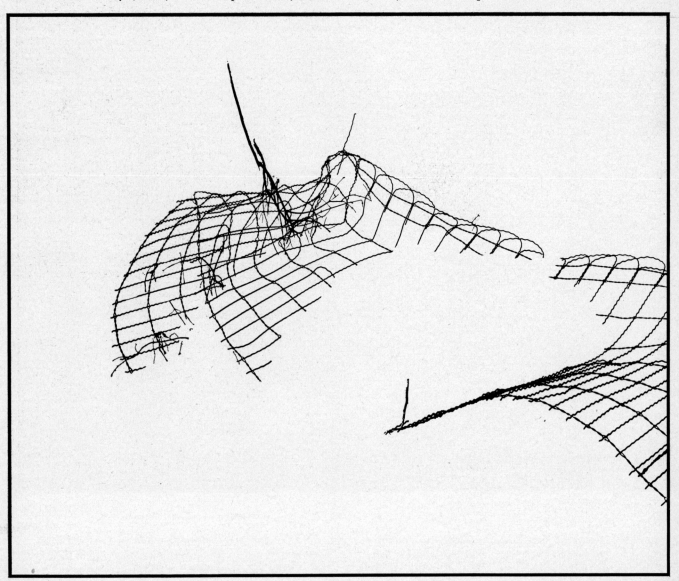

BERNARD DAVIS SUNDAY PAINTER

"This picture," writes Davis, a management consultant by profession, "is one that I made while doing a photo story of Sunday painters in Paris. The elderly lady was painting the church of St. Julien-le-Pauvre near the Notre Dame cathedral." A recent newcomer to photography, Davis' work has been exhibited at the *Museum of Modern Art* in N. Y.

FRITZ HENLE   BEACH NUDE

PAUL BERG   MOTHER AND CHILD

.99

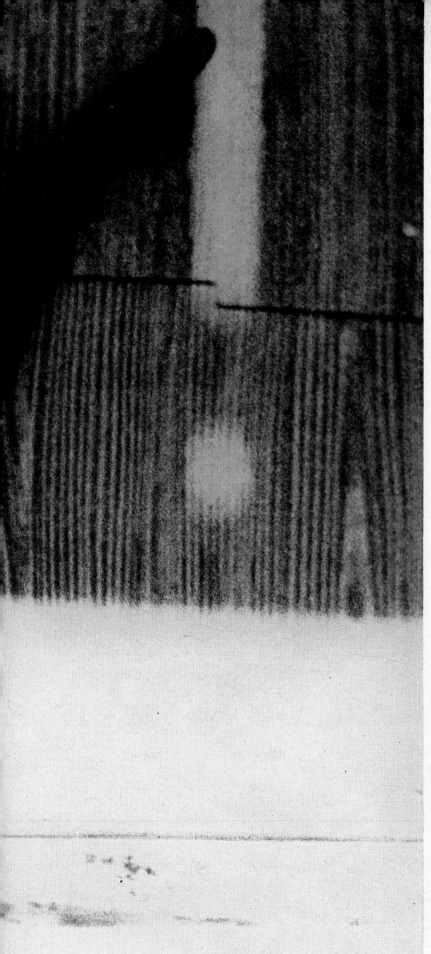

PAUL BERG

MOTHER AND CHILD (PAGE 98)

A staff photographer on the St. Louis *Post-Dispatch* since 1942, Berg made this picture while doing an audience reaction story at a local open-air circus. He used an Automatic Rolleiflex, exposing at 1/250th of a second at f/8 with a #5 synchronized flash-bulb.

FRITZ HENLE

BEACH NUDE (PAGE 99)

To Fritz Henle, famed Rolleiflex photographer, pictures "are the result of a search—a search through which all my visions have been crystallized into images on film." The nude on *page 99* was taken with an Automatic Rolleiflex at 1/100th of a second at f/11.

INGEBORG DE BEAUSACQ

NUDE (PAGE 102)

After studying in Europe, Miss De Beausacq went to Brazil, embarking upon a photographic career that recently brought her to the United States. For the picture on *page 102*, she used an Automatic Rolleiflex, exposing at 1/10th of a second at f/5.6 with floodlights.

HENRY PARKER

CAT ON LEDGE

Parker achieves novel results by his unusual approach to subject matter; he rarely takes a conventionally posed picture. Harsh sunlight accentuated the extreme contrast of the print on the left, which was taken with a Contax at 1/200th of a second on Plus-X film at f/8.

INGEBORG DE BEAUSACQ   NUDE

IRA DOUD, JR.   SOLARIZED STUDY

BILL WITT

"In photographing, I try to see my picture completely, just as it will appear in the finished print, even to the size it will be made, before I snap the shutter." A commercial pho-

IRA DOUD, JR.

Doud's unusual solarized study of a fashion model was made as part of a series of experiments conducted in the noted

BOB TAYLOR

An agricultural photographer, Bob Taylor's picture of some baby chicks resulted from careful planning and patient waiting. Using a green window as a background, Taylor made

tographer in Newark, New Jersey, Witt took both pictures (*above* and to the *right*) with a 4x5 view camera, an 8" coated lens, with two flashbulbs for illumination.

SOLARIZED STUDY (PAGE 103)

photographic workshop of Eddie Kaminski. The picture was made with diffused studio lights and an Automatic Rolleiflex.

CHICKS (PAGES 104-105)

roosts from tubular cardboard. After hours of waiting, the chicks huddled together in the desired manner. A 4 x 5 Graphic view camera with a Wollensak f/4.5 lens was used.

LEONARD McCOMBE

BEACH SCENE (PAGE 108)

Using a Contax camera in an effort to be as unobtrusive as possible McCombe caught the gay spontaneity of the scene on *page 108* while taking a series of pictures with a bathing-beach theme. The exposure was made with high-speed Panchromatic film in bright daylight.

JACK GORMAN

CAT AND MOUSE (PAGE 109)

A staff photographer on the *San Francisco Examiner* since 1945, Gorman attributes the remarkable results of his cat and mouse pictures to "perspiration, perspicacity, plus the normal reactions of two obliging subjects." Three strobe units froze the action, with Gorman using a 4x5 Speed Graphic and Panchro-Press Type-B film. Synchronizing his shutter with the strobe units, Gorman set his f/4.5 Ektar lens to an aperture of f/32 to make this interesting series.

HORST P. HORST

CHAIRS IN A ROMAN COURTYARD

A student of architecture under Le Corbusier, Horst became a *Vogue* photographer twenty years ago, a position which has kept him shuttling between New York and Europe on all types of picture assignments. During the past war, he was a photographer in the U.S. Army Signal Corps. Besides serving as editor of a collection of photographs called *Orientals,* Horst has had two books published; *Photographs of a Decade* and *Patterns from Nature.* Fundamentally he is a romanticist, an "illusionist" with a sculptor's sense of form. His study of a courtyard in Rome was made with an Automatic Rolleiflex camera at an exposure of 1/50th of a second at f/11 on Super-XX.

WILLIAM HUGHES

FISH BOWL

"To me," writes Hughes, "photography is a means of communication, like writing or speaking. If a picture, any picture, doesn't communicate the idea or feeling or mood intended, it is a failure." A student at the Art Center School, Hughes made the exposure with a 4x5 view camera shooting at 1/400th of a second at f/32 with 3 Press 40 flash bulbs.

Audubon

THE PHOTOGRAPHS of Allan Cruickshank and other Audubon Society photographers have been a part of U.S. Camera Annual since its inception. No individual or group has done more in one phase of nature photography—the life, looks and habits of America's birds.

The files of the Audubon Society contain hundreds of examples of professional photography at its best. Every picture is a picture with a purpose; a picture to be published; or to be used in a class room or a reference library. Instead of being commonplace, run-of-the-mill stuff, these are pictures that belong in Annuals, in shows and in the hands and albums of bird lovers everywhere. And not least, but highest among their assets is their ability to make bird-lovers of those of us who prior to seeing the Audubon pictures and publications hadn't given much thought to the subject.

Cruickshank is the only staff photographer the Audubon Society has. All others work on a free-lance basis—many are part-time professionals. George (Continued on Page 400)

NETS

By ELIOT ELISOFON

ELIOT ELISOFON, one of our best photographers, usually graces U.S. Camera's pages with stories of high impact. His world-wide journeys for *Life* magazine usually bring him into contact with major political, humanistic and aesthetic stories throughout the world.

Yet, from the first Elisofon story in U.S. Camera Annual 10 years ago, there has always been either a full or a frustrated sense of gaity and humor lurking somewhere in each job he has done.

This year, his whimsical set of photographs of nets around the world is completely captivating. These

ARCTIC CIRCLE   ATLANTIC COAST

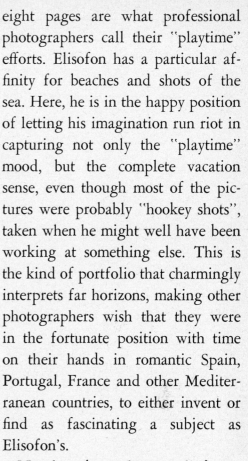

eight pages are what professional photographers call their "playtime" efforts. Elisofon has a particular affinity for beaches and shots of the sea. Here, he is in the happy position of letting his imagination run riot in capturing not only the "playtime" mood, but the complete vacation sense, even though most of the pictures were probably "hookey shots", taken when he might well have been working at something else. This is the kind of portfolio that charmingly interprets far horizons, making other photographers wish that they were in the fortunate position with time on their hands in romantic Spain, Portugal, France and other Mediterranean countries, to either invent or find as fascinating a subject as Elisofon's.

Nets have been photographed over and over and over again. Some photographers like them best as they

FRANCE   SOUTH SPAIN

veil attractive women's faces. Others like them best at work in the sea. Elisofon seems to enjoy them most at rest, a sensation he finds rather enchanting. In the one picture that shows the nets at work, even the fish, frustrated by their position in the net, have decided to take it easy.

It's a wonderful world that Elisofon catches so easily on these eight pages.

In a letter from the Congo in Africa, where he is currently on assignment for *Life,* Elisofon writes: "I photograph nets because they have a delicacy of texture which only the camera can fully exploit and the arrangements made by chance are often interesting in design and form. I have never arranged a net to change its location or composition, not because I am a purist but because I accept the nets as they are, and the challenge they offer. An arrangement

MEXICO   NORWAY

of a net is rarely as good as the one already arranged by chance.

"There is no special technique in photographing nets. I have used three cameras to do this group; a Contax, Rolleiflex, and Linhof Technica. I prefer the Linhof as I have a large group of lenses to choose from, thus better controlling the action and the perspective. The other two cameras were used when they were in hand.

A problem peculiar to net photography is the rendition of sky tones. A good panchromatic film like Super-XX, which I prefer, will render blue sky a light grey if the exposure and development of the film are managed properly. The introduction of filters must be made with care, as the grey of an overcorrected sky can often merge with the mesh of the net. The filter I use most is the K1."

PORTUGAL

MASSACHUSETTS

CHILE

NORTH SPAIN

CARTER **FASHION MODEL**

Carter is a young American who successfully took up photography in Paris a few years ago, and since his return his work has appeared in *Vogue, Life* and *This Week.* The picture above, made on assignment for *Life,* resulted from an attempt at an unconventional fashion shot. He used an Automatic Rolleiflex, exposing at 1/100th of a second at aperture f/3.5.

RICHARD SAUNDERS

TOYS (PAGE 129)

Born in Bermuda, Saunders is presently engaged in a series of projects for the *Photographic Library* of the University of Pittsburgh, under the direction of Roy Stryker, of the *Standard Oil Company* of New Jersey. Before joining Stryker's group, Saunders worked on assignments for *Life, Our World* and *Ebony* magazines. His study on *page 129* was made with a Rolleiflex camera equipped with a f/3.5 Schneider Xenar lens. Using Super-XX, he exposed for 1/100th of a second at f/4.

GENE THOMAS

NAVY WINS

A staff photographer for *Acme Newspictures,* Thomas caught the action on the right just before the kick-off of the 1950 football classic between Army and Navy at Municipal Stadium in Philadelphia. The Navy captain, Tom Bakke and the leader of the Army squad, Dan Foldberg, appear with President Truman. In a startling upset, Navy defeated Army 14-2, thereby ending Army's 28 game winning streak. The picture was one of the award winners at the 1951 White House News Photographers Exhibit.

HARRY CALLAHAN

STUDIES (PAGE 132)

Since 1946 Harry Callahan has been head of the photography department of the *Institute of Design* at the Illinois *Institute of Technology*. A native of Detroit, Callahan studied engineering at *Michigan State* and took up photography in 1938.

In an interview in *Newsweek* magazine last May in connection with an exhibition of his work at the Institute, Callahan said:

"My work is not storytelling. It's not like documentary pictures. It's the subject-matter that counts, but I'm interested in revealing the subject in a new way to intensify it.

"A photo is able to capture a moment that people can't always see with their eyes. It helps you to see more of life around you. Wanting to see more makes you grow as a person, and growing makes you want to show more of life around you."

HARRY CALLAHAN   STUDIES

WILL CONNELL

LEJAREN A. HILLER

"This," writes Connell, "is one of my favorites in the old family album category. It's a happy combination of two of my hobbies, the old album (pushed a trifle beyond the plush-bound standards) and Larry, who needs no pushing either

before or behind the red velvet focusing cloth. Technical data at 2 a.m. is always somewhat hazy. The camera, a mere youngster of *circa* 1936, was a 5 x 7 Ansco View (with 4 x 5 back) on a steady tripod; the lens a 10½" Steinheil Cassar."

MARGARET BOURKE-WHITE

BOMB BAY OF A B-36

One of *Life* magazine's most famous and daring photographers, Margaret Bourke-White has covered the full range of magazine assignment from the charming landscapes of Connecticut to scenes of men at war. Her work has taken her to all parts of the globe, most of which she has covered by air. Starting in 1927 as an industrial photographer, when she photographed the steel mills of Pittsburgh, she has taken photographs in over 30 countries, including the Arctic regions, and she made the first industrial photographs in Soviet Russia to show the progress of the first five-year plan. During the war she was an accredited war correspondent-photographer for *Life* and covered all of the European war theater fronts from 1942 through 1944.

On a recent assignment Miss Bourke-White covered SAC, the Strategic Air Command, which is on 24-hour alert as one of our first weapons of offense in case of attack upon the U.S. The striking photo at left is from this series and shows the open bomb bay of a B-36 at Carswell Field, Texas.

(Photo Life © Time, Inc.)

EDWARD STEICHEN

136

GREEN PASTURES (*From Vanity Fair © 1951, The Condé Nast Publications, Inc.*)

IRVING PENN

COAL MAN

HOUSE PAINTER

COACHMAN

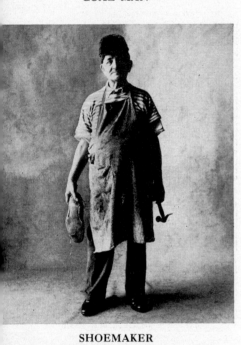

SHOEMAKER

DEEP-SEA DIVER

PNEUMATIC DRILLER

TAXI DRIVER

HEADWAITER

LINEMAN

PLUMBER   BEER LOADER   DAY LABORER

LONGSHOREMAN   ICEMAN   FLOWER DELIVERY BOY

POLICEMAN   MAILMAN   STREET CLEANER

IRVING PENN   NEW YORK SMALL TRADES

140

TOUGH

RUSHING THE GROWLER

EMPLOYEE OF THE GAS COMPANIES

STRAWBERRY VENDOR

THE ICEMAN

RAPID MESSENGER SERVICE

ONE OF THE FINEST

LETTER CARRIER

NICE FEATHER DUSTER

SIGMUND KRAUSZ

STREET TYPES OF CHICAGO, 1891

IRVING PENN

SMALL TRADES (PAGES 138-139)

For many years Irving Penn has been photographing the people engaged in small trades who wear some sort of distinguishing uniform in connection with their work. In the July 1951 issue of *Vogue* were published 60 of his studies taken in New York and those appearing on pages 138-9 are from this series by courtesy of *Condé Nast Publications, Inc.* Penn photographed all of them in his studio under natural daylight.

SIGMUND KRAUSZ

STREET TYPES OF CHICAGO (PAGE 141)

These interesting studies by Sigmund Krausz, until now an unknown photographer, were deposited by him with the Bureau of Copyright of the Library of Congress in 1891, and were recently discovered together with thousands of prints by different photographers, by Paul Vanderbilt, Consultant in Iconography at the Library. They are part of the exhibition of "Forgotten Photographers" which Edward Steichen assembled at the *Museum of Modern Art* in August from a group of more than 10,000 prints that Mr. Vanderbilt had assembled from the files of the Library, covering the period from 1870 to about 1925.

CHARLES KERLEE

CAR TEST

"The four cars," says Kerlee, "were lined up two miles out of the picture area and drove toward the camera at 30 miles per hour. Each car dragged a set of tire chains to produce the dust. The chains were necessary since the cars would have had to be driven 60 miles per hour to raise the right amount of dust." It was taken in the Mojave Desert as an advertisement for the Chrysler Motor Corp.

Kerlee used an 8 x 10 view camera with a 12" Apo Tessar Lens set at f/16 at 1/200th of a second. The picture was made on Super-XX film late in the afternoon.

ROBERT MONROE

HELEN (PAGE 144)

"In this photo I was trying to capture the natural beauty of a woman," says Monroe "to prove that there is beauty behind all the pancake and powder."

Monroe used a Rolleiflex camera. The exposure was for 1/100th of a second at f/16. It was taken on a bright, clear day with sunlight behind the head, and a Proxar lens was used for extreme close-up with Super-XX film.

JACK FIELDS

LION CUB (PAGE 145)

"This," writes Fields "is one of the very few animal pictures that I've taken with the Graphic and flash, as I much prefer a reflex-type camera with strobe."

Fields, who was studying for a Master's degree in biology but decided to become a photographer instead shot the angry lion cub with a 4X5 Speed Graphic with 6" Goerz Dagor lens. The exposure was for 1/100th of a second at f/32 with one flash No. 22 held high above the lion cub's head.

VAL SARRA

SUNDAY AFTERNOON

This charming portrait of a family spending a quiet Sunday afternoon is one of a series which Sarra made for the Eastman Kodak Co. Sarra, one of the top men in the commercial and advertising fields, used an Eastman Kodak Master-View 4X5 camera with an Ektar lens. He made an exposure of 1/75th of a second at f/16 and the film was Kodak Super-XX.

ROBERT J. FLAHERTY, 1884-1951   **W. SUSCHITZKY**

JOHN GRIERSON, wartime chief of the National Film Board of Canada, was a close friend and co-worker of Robert Flaherty. Writing of him in the New York *Times* shortly after his death he beautifully summed up a great man and a great career when he said in part: "Robert Flaherty . . . was one of the great innovators of the screen—an artist who will have his own assured niche in the history of the medium alongside those of George Mélieès, D. W. Griffith, Mack Sennett and Serge Eisenstein. Primarily, his unique contribution was to the visual beauty of the cinema. . . . His talent was lyric; his achievement was simply that he was the first to seize upon the enormous powers of the motion picture camera to observe nature and the natural . . . He had perhaps the most gracious eye that ever guided a camera, and his deathless record is there—in the howling blizzards of 'Nanook of the North,' in the dances of 'Moana,' in the wild storms of 'Man of Aran,' and in the bayou waters of 'The Louisiana Story.' He was a man of enormous charm, taste and distinction of mind . . . and one who threw out more ideas in and about film-making than any one of us had the wit to gather up."

A Spanish Village

By W. EUGENE SMITH

(Courtesy of "Life" Magazine)

THESE photographs are pictorial paragraphs from my portrait of a modest village. I went away from the publicized historical attractions, the unrepresentative disproportion of the main cities: for, away from the tourist landmarks, Spain is to be found. Spain is of its villages, simple down to the poverty line, its people unlazy in slow-paced striving to earn a frugal living from the ungenerous soil. Centuries of the blight of neglect, of exploitation, of the present intense domination, weigh heavily—yet they, as a whole, are not defeated. "They work the day, and sleep the night; struggle for and bake their bread; believing in life, they reluctantly relinquish their dead."

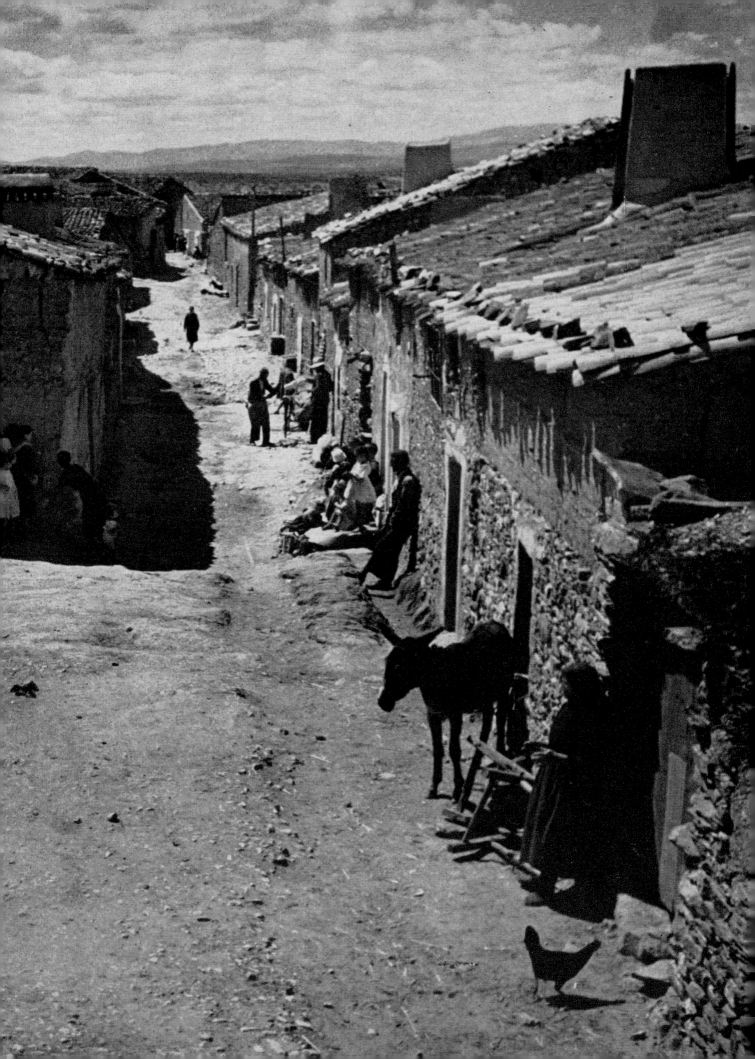

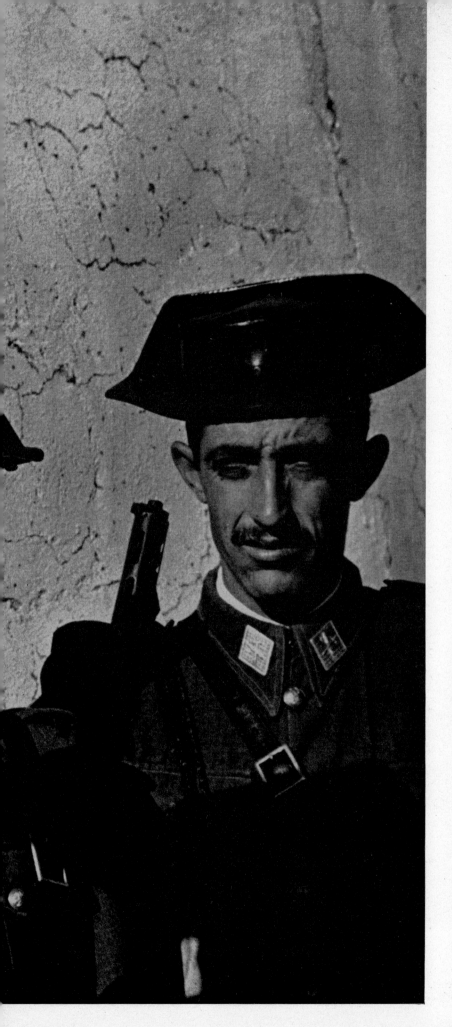

The Guardia Civil (Franco's rural police, so despised and feared by the villagers) came late at night and examined our papers once again. They labored at copying them, including the "fortunate" letter concerning my equipment that they had interpreted as giving me complete official permission to photograph everything. They asked questions concerning dates of arrivals and departures—if we were hesitant they answered for us.

The following day the Falange officials of the village said the letter contained nothing giving us permission to take notes—which they, now, smilingly forbade us to do. We were forbidden to ask any names, any dates, any facts concerning the village. This order was a serious blow to accurate reporting which I naturally had to ignore.

I continued to photograph, aware that we were being watched. We went into homes and, behind closed doors asked questions, hoping our voices would not carry too clearly to the bypassers. Reports came to us that upon our leaving the people were questioned as to what we asked, said, and did. One man who helped us a great deal was put under the eye of a guard, " . . . for another incident." I could not understand why a guard was not assigned to accompany us. It was good that most of the villagers were our friends. I worked slowly, trying carefully to pull a balanced story, trying to tie the loose ends together. Except for the still inadequate caption material I felt one more day would do it.

I was leaning against the wall talking to Nina (the interpreter) through her open door when the Guardia Civil came again, accompanied by a huge unfriendly looking man in civilian clothes. He walked straight to us and without courtesy demanded our papers. He glanced through them, then held Nina's Spanish passport in one hand, kept drumming it against the other. His tone was rough as he questioned her and then the both of us. He tried to trap, he tried to insult, he tried to threaten. He also questioned where the films were, when they would be developed, who would develop them, who would pass upon them. We parried, pacified, threw false scents, said the film was almost all in Madrid (which it was). Abruptly he turned and left, so did the uniformed men.

We stood staring at the emptiness. "Nina, dear child, may I make a slight suggestion— let us pass up our remaining, rather unimportant pictures, and get the hell out of here while you still have your freedom, and I still have my film." Whether the step was necessary or not, we drove all of the night and crossed into France at noon the following day.

The second day we were in the village an old woman walked along with us. Among many things, she said this, "We do not know what you are, some believe you to be Amer- ican journalists. If you are, we ask only of you to speak the truth of what you see." This was rather different from the attitude and the desires of the governing officials.

154

Another time, the man who in my photograph is staring through the doorway into the room in which his father lay in death, concluded a long heart-searching afternoon of exchange with me, "If you could photograph not only our physical life, but also that which is of our heart!" I did not answer, I knew it was impossible, yet this I tried to do.

INTERNATIONAL PHOTOGRAPHY

THE photograph in Europe, Australia and Asia is very little different from the photograph in the U.S.A. as this year's Annual shows. Here are fine individual pictures—here are groups of pictures that compare favorably and variably with those in the American Section. Perhaps the pictures are so similar that the division may well seem arbitrary.

But within the division the pictures are different from those of the last two years. Starting with George Cserna's magnificent cats (*next page*) there is less emphasis on the purely pictorial, more on pictures with people, and animals, and action. That too is why the International Section is so like the American Section.

The Jean Manzon shots from Rome, Brazil, and France (*pages 184, 205, 222, 223*) are the work of a very fine craftsman who seems at home in any human or geographical area of the globe. The Emil Brunner aerial shots of the Sahara (*pages 238-241*) are unique—a precise pattern of villages and oases from the air that startle the observer with their abstract quality, yet are so real the interpretive force is astonishing. This is one of the year's best photo works. Frank Hurley's Australian pictures (*pages 226-231*) are wonders of another kind—realism taken to the border of fantasy. This photographer captures heroic pictures—vast canvasses that show nature at its most romantic The Japanese pictures portray the work of a nation that seems dedicated to and enchanted by photography. Though small this is a vital section representing a country that is so photogenic in both people and places. The bird pictures of Roy Kurokawa (*page 212*); the burlesque night club photo of Jun Yoshida (*page 208*)—what fine food and foolery shots these are. We have asked Horace Bristol, former *Life* photographer, who since World War II has his own photo agency and publishing business in Tokyo, for his opinions on photography in Japan today. He writes as follows:

"The over-all picture of Japanese photography in 1951 is somewhat fuzzy and slightly out-of-focus, for this island of avid amateur and rabid professional photographers hasn't quite made up its mind as to what it expects of postwar photography.

"Whatever it lacks in focus on an ultimate objective, it certainly cannot be called under-exposed as to subject matter (whether it is under-developed or not is a matter of personal preference)—for Japanese photographers have definitely discovered the human body as a prime photographic target. After centuries of bathing together in perfect indifference (artistic or otherwise) to the nude female body, it is now the center of interest, for better or worse.

"Not all have been works of art, by any judgment, but this is probably only a passing phase; already there has been some slight swing of the pendulum away from this rather noticeable emphasis on nakedness. However, the chances of Japanese photographers returning to taking misty scenes of Mt. Fuji at twilight are rather remote, at this writing. For whatever else the current photographic scene discloses, it is full of life and vitality. While no definitely Japanese school of photography has as yet emerged since the war (most photographers are too busy copying every popular trend in America and Europe), there is a wonderful feeling of robustness and innocence about the present-day Japanese photographic world.

"For the moment, they are unduly preoccupied with imitating men like Irving Penn, Karsh, or Henri Cartier-Bresson, to name a few of the most influential forces at work on the advanced amateur and professional. Philippe Halsman and Andre de Dienes are also much admired, which means copied, for the Japanese know no more sincere form of admiration than mimicry, but this is little more than an indication of the great ferment which seems to be stirring in the Japanese photographic world today.

"Regardless of the fact that neither film, paper, or cameras are really cheap by comparison to Japanese living costs, camera production and camera ownership have soared to almost fantastic proportions. Although ninety percent of the cameras sold and used in Japan are of the less expensive types, similar to box brownies of simple reflex equipment, the sign of a genuine enthusiast among amateurs is no longer a shiny chromium *German* camera. Today the mark of the current generation of amateurs is the possession of a made-in-Japan Nikon or Canon.

"But one fact predominates the photographic scene in Japan:—photography today is a dynamic thing, and the Japanese are applying their boundless energy as well as imitative ability in developing a truly creative art of their own."

The individual pictures have much more variety than last year's: Aart Klein's zebra on page 202 and his marching generations on 203 are a particularly fortunate pairing. There are still mountains that are awesome, enchanting vistas of forests and flowers. But it's the people—Swiss, German, French, Scandinavian that color and add a humanity and gaiety that are welcome attractions.

If fault can be found with this Section it should be found with the editors. We still are not doing justice to pictures around the world because we haven't pursued them literally around the world. Editing from New York is editing from the best center in either hemisphere. But really getting the widest variety of material means forsaking headquarters and roaming the width and length of all the countries where photography is important—and that means everywhere. The best photo feat of the year, so perfectly reproduced in *Life* was the color story of twenty-four hours—by the hour—of the sun. The panorama of an Arctic day was photographed from a tiny island off the northwest coast of Norway by two Swiss photographers, Emil Schulthess and Emil Spühler, whose dramatic panorama appears on *pages 9-17*.

All over the world are other interesting photo adventures. We see too few of them and discontentedly go to press knowing not the photographers but the editors are remiss.

—TOM MALONEY

CATS

by GEORGE CSERNA

GEORGE CSERNA, a young hungarian-born photographer now free-lancing in New York,
spent the post-war years photographing in Switzerland. He worked in various photo studios in
Lausanne and in Brussels prior to coming to
America last spring.

The interesting photographs of cats on the following ten pages were made as a joint effort with

Henri Saas, a Swiss photographer with whom Cserna worked in Lausanne. Some of the photographs have appeared in a book of cats, recently published in Switzerland, and Cserna's work has been published in the Swiss *Camera* magazine.

"One evening," says Cserna, "Saas and I developed an idea to photograph cats . . . a whole series of them. We looked in the Lausanne telephone book and found the address of a place where thoroughbred cats were bred, trained and sold.

"After a visit to the house and obtaining permission to photograph, we returned with our equipment and planned to take the pictures we wanted in a few hours. But we had planned without considering the moods and temperaments of the cats. Instead of a few hours, it took us several days.

"Our equipment consisted of a couple of Rolleiflexes and one strobe unit which was used off-camera. Several technical problems arose. The light had to be used above the cats, otherwise the eyes lost all their luminosity and looked like shoe-buttons. Almost each cat—and there were twenty of them, mainly grey and blue Persians— had a personality all its own. There were days when it was impossible to do anything because of a complete lack of cooperation between model and photographer, at which times even bribes of fragrant sausage were to no avail.

"Another problem was a common one familiar to all photographers of children with the mothers present at the sitting. The two old ladies who trained the cats were forever combing, brushing and trying to "pose" their charges in the manner they preferred. Fortunately, the reflex camera permits a certain amount of directional deception. An interesting footnote is that the strobe, being so fast, did not bother the cats, but the sound of the shutter did. In all, we took over 200 pictures."

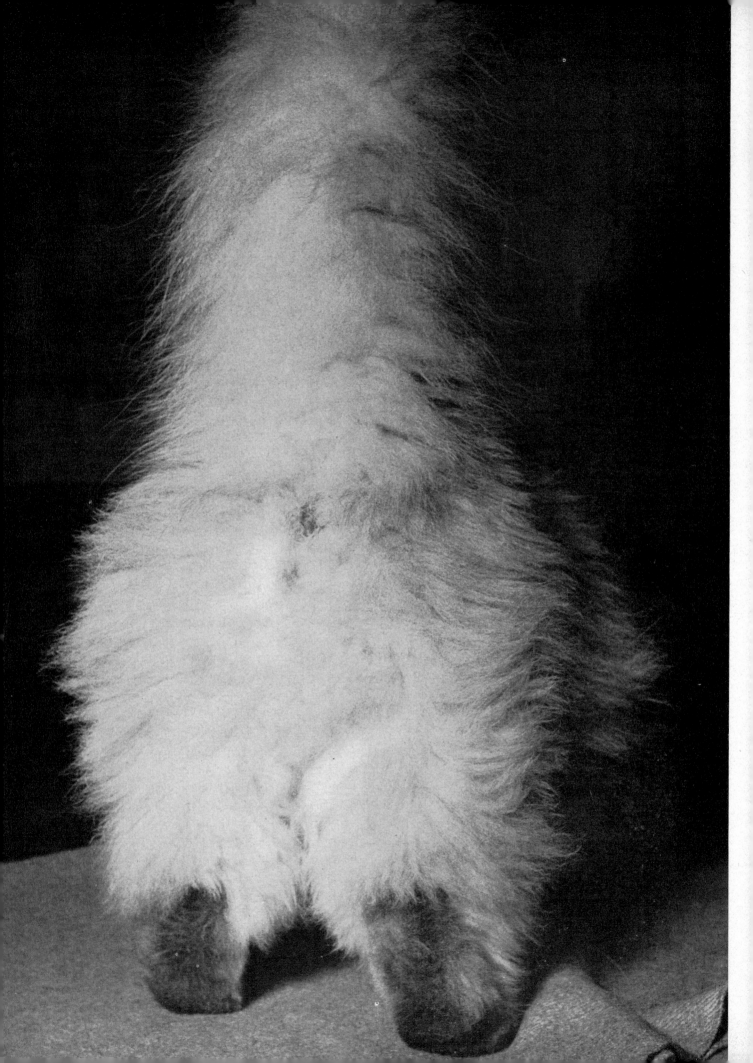

STEN DIDRIK BELLANDER, SWEDEN

CYCLISTS

MAX KOLB, SWITZERLAND

ALPINE LANDSCAPE (PAGE 171)

BERTIL FORSEN, SWEDEN

GOALIE

ALBERT STEINER, SWITZERLAND   WINTER LANDSCAPES ON LAKE ST. MORITZ

ADALBERT DEFNER, AUSTRIA   WINTER·FOREST

ERGY LANDAU, FRANCE

NEW-BORN CALF

BOHUSLAV BURIAN, CZECHOSLOVAKIA   WINDOW CLEANER

GUSTAV HANSSON, SWEDEN   (LANDSCAPES PAGES 180, 181)

GEORGES VIOLLON, FRANCE

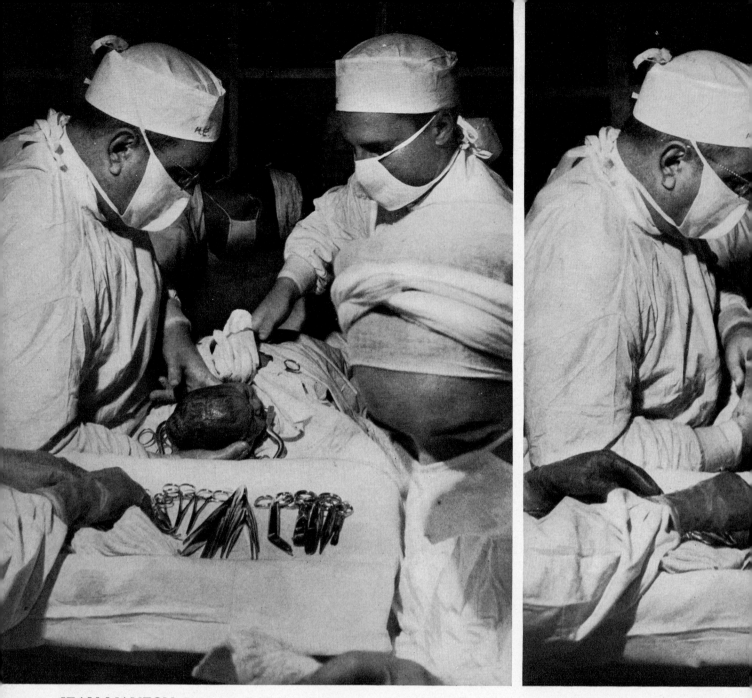

JEAN MANZON, FRANCE

PAUL & JEAN PICHONNIER, BELGIUM

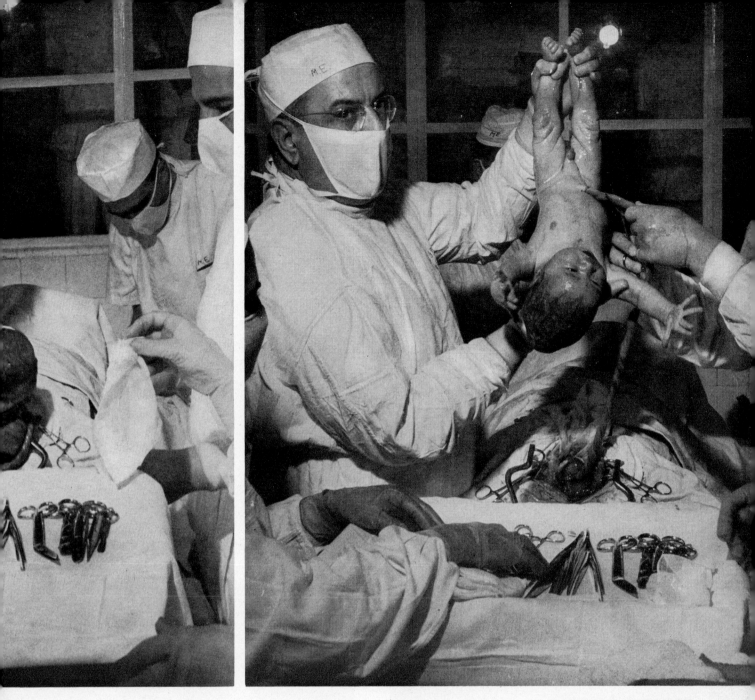

CAESAREAN OPERATION

BRUSSELS (PAGES 186-187)

GEIGER, FRANCE

MARKET WOMAN

ROBERT DOISNEAU, FRANCE

YACHTING ENTHUSIAST

JACQUES ROUCHON, FRANCE

SOLITARY OLD AGE

SAVITRY FRANCE

SEATED NUDE

AXEL POIGNANT, AUSTRALIA											KANGAROO

SIEGFRIED LAUTERWASSER, GERMANY						SWISS ELECTIONS (PAGES 192-193)

194

GEORGE SCHMIDT, GERMANY

NATURE PATTERNS

SERGE DE SAZO, FRANCE   GIRL DIVERS

Serge de Sazo, one of France's most prolific magazine contributors, made these interesting underwater studies near the Iles du Levant, standing at a depth of four to five feet in the Mediterranean Sea. A specially constructed water-tight unit housed his Automatic Rolleiflex, with the exposures made at 1/100th of a second at an aperture of f/5.6 on Super-XX Panchromatic film. A native of Paris, de Sazo specializes in night club and theatrical photography. His work has been published throughout Europe and in American art and photography journals, as well as in national publications, both here and abroad.

W. SUSCHITZKY, ENGLAND

BICYCLE SHOP

ANGEL GARMENDIA, MEXICO

PENITENTS (PAGES 200-201)

W. SUSCHITZKY, ENGLAND

ALMOND TREE

AART KLEIN, HOLLAND

ZEBRA & VACATIONERS (PAGES 202-203)

RELANG, GERMANY

MODEL

JEAN MANZON, FRANCE   MISTINGUETT

RYUICHI AMANO, JAPAN   PENDULUM LIGHT PATTERNS

BRUNO STEFANI, ITALY   LAGO DI GARDA

YOSHIDA, JAPAN   TOKYO NIGHTCLUB

NAKAFUJI, JAPAN   BUDDHA

SENZO YOSHIOKA, JAPAN

WINDY DAY

SENZO YOSHIOKA, JAPAN WRESTLER

ROY KUROKAWA, JAPAN

FEEDING TIME

213

SENZO YOSHIOKA, JAPAN

BLIZZARD IN TOKYO

MAX KUTTEL, SWITZERLAND   LOURDES

ARMIN HAAB, SWITZERLAND   HORSES (PAGES 216-217)

MAX KUTTEL, SWITZERLAND   SWISS BOYS

ADOLF MORATH, ENGLAND   HANDS (PAGE 220)

JEAN MANZON, FRANCE   THE VATICAN

E. A. HEINIGER, SWITZERLAND   ALPINE LANDSCAPES (PAGE 221)

JEAN MANZON, FRANCE   BRAZILIAN NATIVES

BERINGER & PAMPALUCHI, SWITZERLAND   SLALOM TRAIL (PAGE 224)

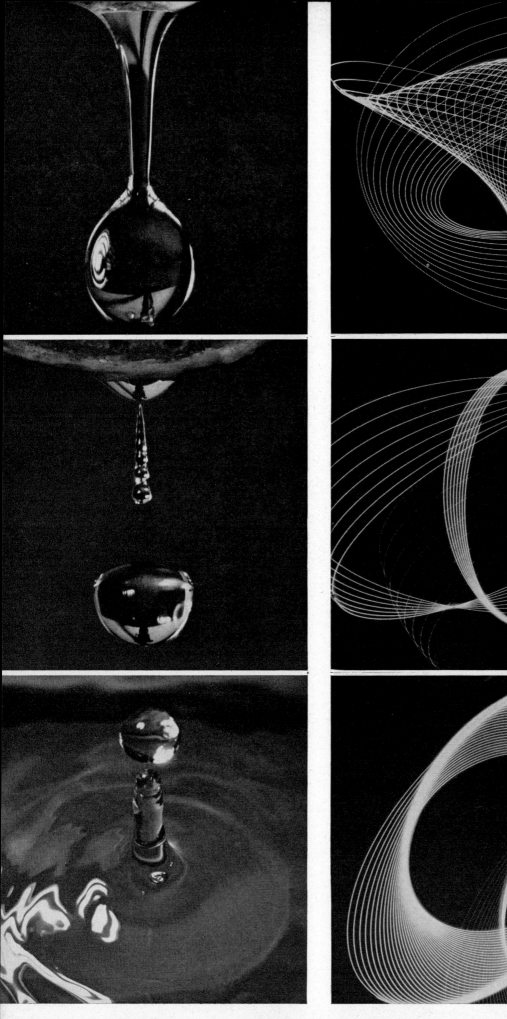
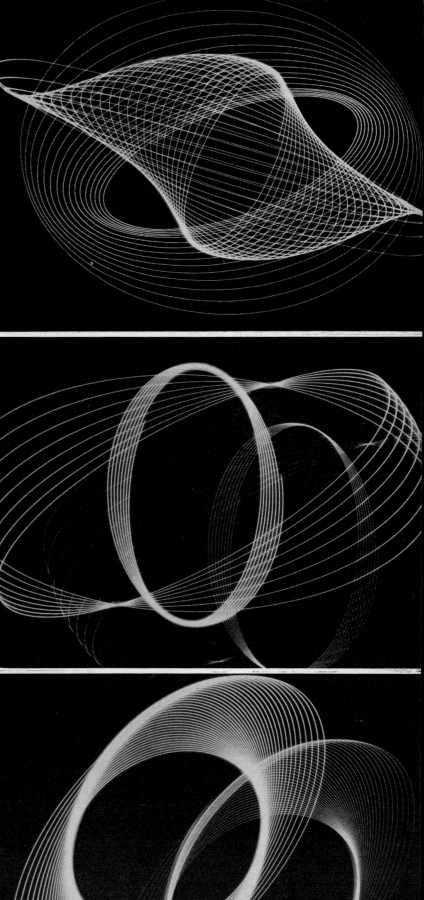

OSKAR KREISEL, GERMANY

PETER KEETMAN, GERMANY

FRANK HURLEY, AUSTRALIA

SEA LIONS, SOUTH GEORGIA

HORACE BRISTOL, U. S. A.

An American photographer, who since the war has been living and working in the Far East, Horace Bristol went into photography professionally in 1930. From 1937 until 1941 he was on *Life's* staff which he left to go into Service as a Navy photographer. He spent 3½ years of the war with Captain Edward Steichen's photographic unit out in the Pacific. After his discharge from the Navy he returned to *Fortune* Magazine on foreign assignment in the Far East.

NIKKO TEMPLES IN THE FOG

About a year later, deciding to make Tokyo his permanent base of operation, Bristol formed his own photographic agency, EAST-WEST, and has also published several books, including one on Korea, and his most recent "Bali-In Pic- tures," now available in this country through U.S. CAM- ERA PUBLISHING CORP. The two photographs (*above*) of Japanese worshippers at the Nikko temples were taken with a Rolleiflex camera at f/3.5 in 1/100th of a second.

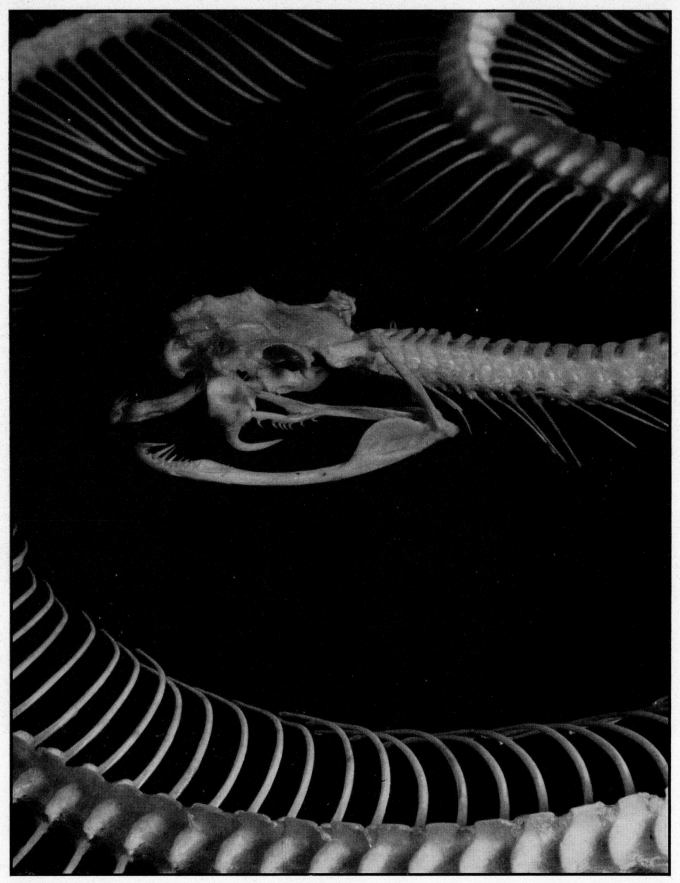

GEORGE RADO, BRAZIL SNAKE SKELETON

ADOLF MORATH, ENGLAND GEORGE BERNARD SHAW

234

HENRI CARTIER-BRESSON, FRANCE   WOMEN OF INDIA

WERNER BISCHOF, SWITZERLAND   ITALIAN BOY

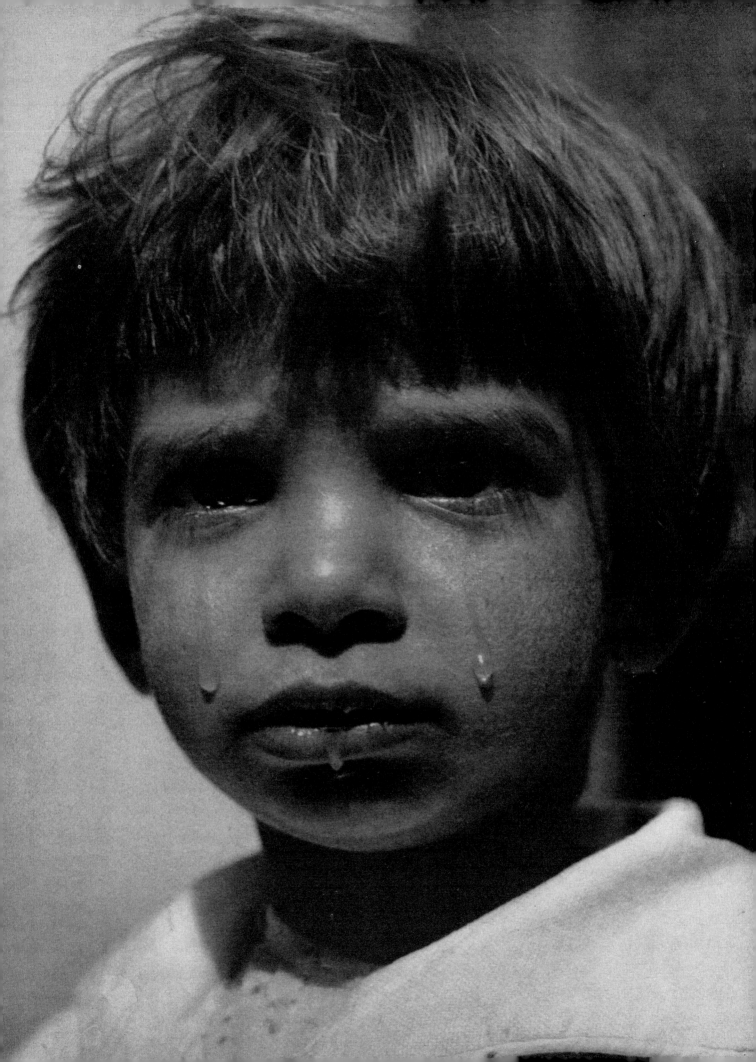

SAHARA

By EMIL BRUNNER

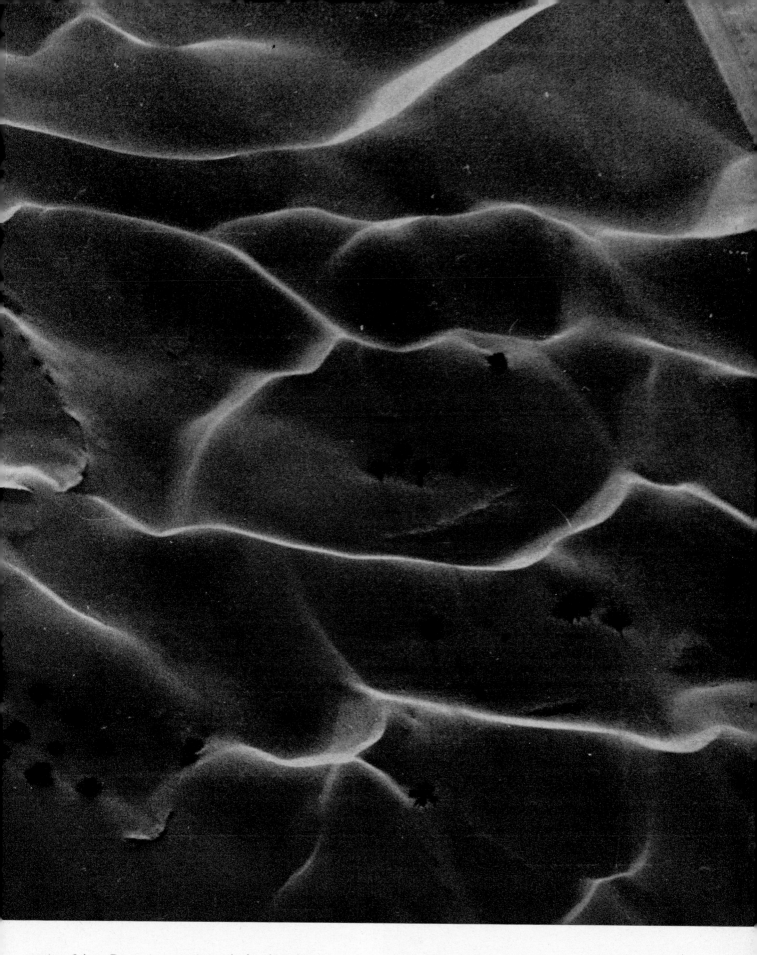

THE Sahara Desert is more than a body of sand, it is an ever-moving mass of dunes, a home to people with little opportunity for change. Emil Brunner, Swiss photographer, in making these aerial views, is more than an expert craftsman, for he captures the utter desolation, the occasional greenness and the thriving life amidst sterile desert sands.

239

THE GREAT Oriental Erf in Algeria is an oasis that is slowly being buried under the ever-present driving force of windswept sand-dunes. Thousands of similar plantations and gardens spots have been developed, only to fall victim to the constantly changing, never-ending sand drifts.

THE SYMMETRY of these beautifully-tended gardens, protected by a wall and hedges, in the eastern part of the Sahara testify to the carefully planned techniques that must be adopted in order to offset desert conditions. The draw well in the background provides water for the gardens.

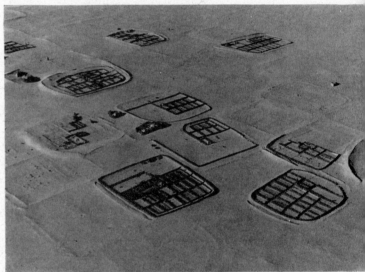

A NARROW camel path is the only link that connects this small oasis with the outside world. There are literally thousands of minute oases scattered over the eastern wastes of the Sahara Desert. Some have been havens for weary travelers for many years; others are buried under in months.

PICTURED HERE are 10 desert gardens in the Great Oriental Erf, in Algeria. Each garden has at least one well for irrigation dug to a depth averaging more than 40 feet. Outlines of old sand-covered gardens can be seen in the vast desolated outlying areas, victims of past sand storms.

EL OUED, a desert town in Algeria, with oriental bazaars and age-old customs, has undergone little change through the passing years. The 10,000 inhabitants of Arabic descent live in small houses made of brown mud-brick, with peculiar cupolas, which are painted white or flamingo-red.

THE PALM trees in this plantation reach heights of 80-90 feet and are protected from driving sands by walls 100-160 feet high; yet, there remains the threat of being swept by sand dunes that have been known to completely cover over similar plantations as they shift across the desert.

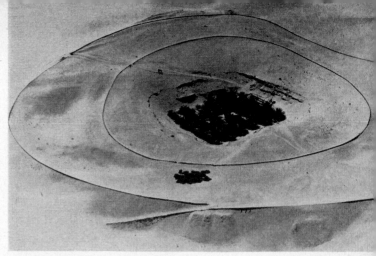

AN AERIAL VIEW of a village possessing its own Mosque, located in the Great Oriental Erf, in Algeria. The tall palm trees lie in cavernous sand craters; a flourishing vegetable garden is to be seen in the upper left hand corner. The village can be reached only by camel caravan.

THE SMALL OASIS shown above is typical of many fruitful spots found in the eastern part of the Sahara Desert. An Arab with his mule can be seen walking along the camel path leading out of the oasis. Bushels of camel fodder are shown growing inside the outer ring of the plantation.

THE SCATTERED Arabian settlement photographed above lies in the vicinity of N'Gouga, Algeria. The small palm tree plantations and tiny vegetable gardens are protected by high walls of sand to ward off the ever-present threat of shifting desert sand dunes and violent sand storms.

THE 160-FOOT walls that surround oases in the desert give them the appearance of volcanic craters when viewed from the air. These are two of 1500 new oases projected by the French government as part of an irrigation plan in the vicinity of the Tripolitanian-Libyan border of Algeria.

BELOW IS A new palm tree plantation on the northern side of the Djebel Toubkal in Morocco. In a few years these palms will bear large quantities of fruit and will continue yielding an abundant crop for over 70 years. Each of the holes (palm nests) contains young date palms.

THIS VIEW IS of a larger settlement in the Sahara. The oasis is protected by three walls, diminishing in size as they near the center of the settlement. The Arab inhabitants raise their own vegetables and camel fodder in gardens located between the outside and middle walls.

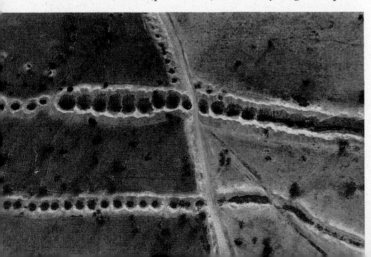

U.S. MARINE   DAVID D. DUNCAN, *Life © Time, Inc.*

ACCENT ON ASIA

THE NEWS this year centers on a focal point of great urgency—Korea. Each day's happenings were of greater or lesser importance as they were within or without the shadow of our fighting forces. This was the spearhead, the thermometer of our open efforts to keep the Kremlin contained on another front.

A truce effort is under way. Even as we most hopefully await the cease fire, we know that with this enemy such a compromise on one front always means a shifting to another.

There will be no ending—the cold war is as constant a reality as each day's rotation of this planet.

U. S. Camera's news highlights this year are mainly those associated with the conflict in Korea. There are pictures of great events, great personalities, great effort to put our country on a plane of security through reorganization of our unparalleled productive facilities. There are also pictures of the great infamy of traitors who would doom a free world to aid a communistic one.

JAKOB MALIK   LEONARD McCOMBE, LIFE

The first major break in the war in Korea occurred on Sept. 15-16, 1950 when UN forces made their first amphibious assault at the port of Inchon. From June 25, when the North Koreans first attacked across the 38th Parallel, until the attack on Inchon the South Koreans and United Nations forces had been able to engage only in desperate holding actions along an ever-shrinking perimeter around Pusan on the southeastern coast.

With insufficient troops to effect an extended break-through from the Pusan bridgehead, Gen. Douglas MacArthur resorted to daring tactics which were employed with such brilliant success in the Pacific during World War II. The plan was to attack the exposed seacoast flanks of the enemy. For tactical and psychological reasons, Seoul, the capital and communications center of South Korea was selected. The capture of Seoul meant that the enemy's main supply lines to his armies in the south would be cut.

An invasion fleet of 261 vessels was assembled to put ashore an estimated 40,000 U. S. Marines, Army troops and South Korean troops. Two days before the assault, 4 U. S. destroyers were sent in to draw pointblank fire from the shore batteries surrounding Inchon, mostly on Wolmi Island. The Reds gave away their defense positions, and for two days. Wolmi and Inchon were battered by the guns and planes of the fleet.

U. S Marines, equipped with scaling ladders, seized Wolmi and a causeway connecting it to Inchon, after which the rest of the Marine First Division and South Korean Marines landed. The U. S. Army 7th Division followed ashore Sept. 16. Despite the many hydrographic difficulties (the port of Inchon has 30-foot tides) the landing was brilliantly and successfully executed.

One of two tank-led U. S. Marine columns sent toward Seoul reached the northwest suburbs on Sept. 20, after capturing Kimpo airfield and crossing the Han river. The crossing of the Han was supported at long range by the U. S. battleship *Missouri,* which had entered the Korean war by shelling Samchok on the east coast Sept. 15, and had then raced around the peninsula to Inchon and turned its 16-inch guns on the Reds near Seoul.

Invasion commanders under Gen. MacArthur were: Rear Adm. Doyle, who directed the amphibious assault; Maj. Gen. Almond, who commanded the drive on Seoul; and 10th Corps Division commanders, Maj. Gen. Smith of Marine First and Maj. Gen. Barr of Army 7th.

STREET FIGHTING IN SEOUL

MAX DESFOR, *Wide World*

245

Despite the initial success of the landing at Inchon the battle for Seoul was a lot tougher than had been anticipated. U.S. Marines fought their way into the center of the city in a three day battle begun on Sept. 24. Two days later the enemy's main garrison started to flee in disorder to the north but many suicidal Communists were still barricaded in the city, especially in its northeastern sections.

The U.S. Marine First Division, stalled several days by Communists entrenched in caves on a hill west of Seoul, first entered the southwestern part of the city on Sept. 24. As a result of infiltration tactics, the city had to be cleared block by block, in bitter, close-in fighting. By Sept. 27, Marines had raised the American flag over the recaptured U.S. Embassy and flags of the Republic of Korea were flying over the fire-damaged Duk Soo Palace, and the city had been secured.

Meanwhile, a motorized column of U.S. Army First Cavalry troops raced 55 miles north from the ballooning "beachhead" in southeastern Korea to link up with the 7th Division below Seoul, closing a trap on an estimated 35,000 floundering Communist troops in southwestern Korea. The fall of Seoul broke the back of the North Koreans' drive to the south, and was to lead to Red China's entry into the war under the disguise of "volunteers."

HELPING WOUNDED MARINE

MAX DESFOR, *Wide World*

GI RESCUES RABBIT

STANLEY TRETICK, *Acme*

Out of the flaming ruins of a bombed and deserted village an American trooper of the First Cavalry Division dashes out with a live rabbit. Stanley Tretick, former Marine Corps photographer during World War II, does not report on the ultimate fate of the animal.

AIR-DROP (PAGE 250-1)

CARL MYDANS, LIFE © *Time, Inc.*

THE first major use of airborne troops in the Korean war took place Oct. 20, when the 11th Airborne Division dropped some 4,100 men (*left*) about 33 miles north of the North Korean capital of Pyongyang in an attempt to cut off Red troops retreating from the capital. The operation was personally supervised by Gen. MacArthur from his Constellation *SCAP* over the jump area. The following day 1,800 more paratroopers were dropped as reinforcements, as well as tons of supplies, including jeeps and howitzers.

Air power has played a vital though not decisive role in the Korean war. Strategic bombing has struck crippling blows at vital supply lines, marshalling yards, assembly areas, and the industrial centers of North Korea. For political reasons the Manchurian bases and supply depots, where most of the Korean supply lines originate, have not been attacked, and with cheap, abundant manpower, the Reds have been able to keep their troops supplied at the front. From most reports, the tactical support of the front-line elements has been excellent, though the problem of battle control (air *vs* ground force control) remains one to be wrangled over by the Brass in the Pentagon.

But the lessons of the Berlin air-lift have not been forgotten, and a major factor in our ability to remain in Korea in the early days of the war with only a small holding force was due to the application of those principles learned there. Men and equipment were able to be shuttled along a 5,000 mile supply line, air-drops allowed the resupply of units that were encircled, and rapid air evacuation of the wounded has become standard routine, with the helicopter, a newcomer to the battlefield, doing heroic duty.

At the same time, new developments in the form of airplanes of greater cargo-carrying capacity, especially designed for quick loading and unloading of large and heavy pieces of equipment, new and larger parachutes, and special cushioning platforms to prevent damage on landing have greatly expanded the horizons of airborne operations.

BEHIND ENEMY LINES

MAX DESFOR, *Wide World*

SOUTH KOREAN REFUGEES JOE SCHERSCHEL, LIFE © *Time, Inc.*

PARATROOPER STEPS INTO SPACE JOHN DOMINIS, LIFE © *Time, Inc.*

REFUGEES

MAX DESFOR, WIDE WORLD

IN the dramatic photograph (*left*) Max Desfor, *Associated Press'* ace photographer and *Pulitzer Prize* winner, has caught all of the dramatic frenzy of a horde fleeing from danger. They are civilians from Pyongyang, North Korean capital, who, driven by fear of Communist reprisals as our troops withdraw, are scrambling over the twisted girders of a bombed-out bridge over the Taedong River.

At the right, Carl Mydans, *Life* photographer and veteran of many wars, has moved in close and singled out the individual—a little Korean mother seeking safety for a few prized possessions. With her child nursing at her breast, her wedding band on her finger, and a pot, a few old clothes, and a wash basin on her head, she seeks escape from the brutality and waste of war with courage, determination and great pride.

REFUGEES

CARL MYDANS, LIFE © *Time, Inc.*

CHINESE PEOPLES' "VOLUNTEER"   DAVID DOUGLAS DUNCAN, LIFE © *Time, Inc.*

COMMUNIST PRISONERS OF WAR, KOREA   CARL MYDANS, LIFE © *Time, Inc.*

A TELEGRAM FROM THE ARMY

OLLIE NOONAN, *Boston American*

Mrs. Johanna Fowler of Roxbury, Mass., receives word that her son, Alvyn, has been killed in combat in Korea. In World War II she lost another son in the Battle of the Bulge.

The Korean "incident", up to the time of the truce talks, resulted in 75,428 U.S. casualties. There were 12,670 dead, 51,919 wounded, and 10,680 missing. (*International Photo.*)

CONFERENCE ON WAKE ISLAND

ALFONSO A. MUTO, INP

The picture at the left shows President Truman and Gen. Douglas MacArthur at their long-awaited, much-discussed meeting at Wake Island on Oct. 15. Here, along the bloody Japanese invasion beaches of 1941, the President and the head of the UN forces met face to face for the first time. They had not come together to mastermind a plan of attack to rid Korea of the Communists; President Truman simply wanted to get Gen. MacArthur's personal views on the Far Eastern situation. They talked alone for an hour and then held a two-hour staff conference. By 10 a.m. the historic meeting was over. The President issued a communique calling the talks "highly satisfactory." Before he left for Hawaii and the States, Truman pinned a medal on MacArthur.

Many observers believed the meeting was nothing more

than a political maneuver on the President's part with elections close at hand. The meeting of the soldier and the politician for the first time would make the administration and the Armed Forces appear to be working smoothly together. Others felt that the war was just about over, because of MacArthur's assurance the Chinese Reds would not intervene, and the President wanted to confer with him in person about the policy of rehabilitation, since the U. S. has such a large stake in the outcome of UN decisions in Korea.

Six months later, on April 11, after the Administration and MacArthur had drifted farther and farther apart, President Truman dismissed the UN Commander for violating Administration and UN policy. This pleased the UN, but started a violent, though short-lived controversy in the U. S.

WOULD-BE ASSASSIN, WOUNDED

BRUCE G. HOERTEL, NEW YORK TIMES

OSCAR COLLAZO, shown above, got as far as the steps of Blair House in Washington; Griselio Torresola was killed yards away. The first attempt on President Truman's life by assassins was foiled by quick-thinking and resourceful guards. Walking quietly down Pennsylvania Avenue, the two men, Puerto Rican Nationalists, approached Blair House from opposite directions. Collazo reached the steps, where Pvt. Donald Birdzell stood with his back to the street, drew a German Walther P-38 pistol and fired at Birdzell. Instead of shooting back, the guard ran into the street to draw fire away from the house. Guards Boring and Davidson, with Birdzell, opened fire on Collazo who fell, wounded in the chest, at the foot of the steps.

Meanwhile, Torresola began firing with a Luger on guards Leslie Coffelt and Joseph Downs who were in a guard

booth on the west side of Blair House. He wounded both guards, emptied his magazine and turned to jump a low boxwood hedge. He was killed instantly by a bullet in the brain. Leslie Coffelt died four hours later.

The President was awakened from a nap in Blair House by the sound of the firing, rushed to a window to look out. A guard looked up and shouted, "Get back! Get back!" Half an hour later, President Truman left Blair House for a scheduled memorial service for the late Sir John Dill, at Arlington National Cemetery.

Torresola and Collazo, both residents of the Bronx, were found to be workers for the Nationalists. Collazo was charged with the murder of Coffelt, tried in Washington. He was found guilty of murder in the first degree, and sentenced to be electrocuted on October 26, 1951.

PRESIDENT TRUMAN

IN several measures which he signed, President Truman wrote into law some tremendous expenditures for defense, a $190 million loan to India to buy grain, and the new draft law. But even overshadowing the vital legislation of this crucial year, were the President's writings in another vein. He became the center of a storm of denunciation when he wrote to Rep. McDonough a letter in which he said, "The Marine Corps is the Navy's police force and as long as I am President that is what it will remain. They have a propaganda machine that is almost equal to Stalin's." The letter was inserted in the *Congressional Record* by McDonough— then the heat was on. One week later, in an unprecedented action, the President apologized handsomely to the Marines, and to everyone else concerned.

In another of his now-famous letters, President Truman seemed to forget that men who assume high office must of necessity give up most of their privacy. The Washington *Post's* music critic Paul Hume wrote a review about Margaret Truman in which he said that the President's daughter was "flat a good deal of the time" and had no "professional finish." Wrote the President to the critic: "I have just read your lousy review . . . I never met you, but if I do you'll need a new nose. . . . "

In the photo above, Harry S. Truman is shown as he "reluctantly" signed the new economic control bill on July 31. The dour-looking President charged that the bill was gravely deficient, and would encourage the return of the black markets. But probably the most controversial paper signed by the President all year, was the order which relieved Gen. MacArthur of his commands in the Far East.

GENERAL WALKER'S BODY COMES HOME   BOB MULLIGAN, INTERNATIONAL

MARINES RETREAT FROM CHOSEN RESERVOIR   MAX DESFOR, WIDE WORLD

THAT the Navy is still our first line—of defense and offense, has been shown in Korea. While theoreticians and experts dwell on the likelihood that another war would see air power used the way sea power was used in World War II, the Navy carries out, under the very nose of the enemy, a galling, little-noticed but important engagement.

Air power undoubtedly will be able to deliver airborne assaults in force, but the Navy showed at Inchon that sea-borne assaults are still a tremendously powerful force. The Navy showed a new trick, too—at Hungnam, the retreating forces were carried to the beaches by units of the Seventh Fleet, not in another Dunkerque, but with brilliant maneuvering that looked like "Inchon in reverse".

The leaders of the Navy realize the necessity for an "offensive-minded" approach to their problems. Hence, they are building up a trained, mobile and versatile striking force, ready for operation on slight notice. They are developing new ships and weapons with the first achievements of the "atomic age" built into them. Twelve *Essex*-class carriers have been or are being modernized to carry jet-propelled atom bombers; submarines have been re-designed to permit them to fire (presumably atomic) guided missiles. And perhaps the biggest Navy news of the year was the announcement that plans are going ahead for the development and building of an atomic energy-powered submarine, with a power plant to be delivered by the Atomic Energy Commission.

The Navy's eye on defensive building included such steps as rebuilding nearly a score of destroyers and submarines to serve as radar picket boats off the U. S. coasts; the new luxury liners *Independence, Constitution* and *United States* have all been built with troopship conversion strongly in mind.

With suggestions that the Navy be renamed "The U. S. Air Navy" indicating the growth of strength within the Department itself in air-power thinking—with the demothballing of nearly two hundred ships laid up after the last war—and with the new developments proceeding at a dizzy pace, we can be assured that whatever mothballs had accumulated within the Navy Department's offices were also being cleared away.

U.S.S. MANCHESTER,

LT. KENNETH HENRY, U.S. NAVY

FAREWELLS

The war in Korea was first brought home to many Americans by the loss of sons or husbands in battle; it was suddenly made closer to thousands more as their loved ones left home for training camps, for shipboard service, for the fighting area.

Ralph Crane's sympathetic camera recorded one of war's most poignant scenes: the dockside farewell. Shown on these pages are a few of the officers and men of the carrier, *Philip-*

pine Sea (named for a great battle of the last war), saying their good-byes before the ship sailed into the Pacific; this is a moving but tragic record of war.

Barring all-out war, the Navy plans to call up approximately 6,000 Reserve officers, most of whom will come from

the Organized Reserve Pool which contains a list of about 15,000 officers, and about 1,000 to 2,000 will come from the 235,000 officers left in the Volunteer Reserve.

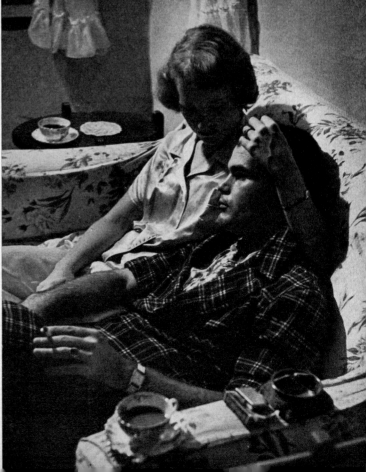

GENERAL GEORGE C. MARSHALL

PHILIPPE HALSMAN, LIFE © *Time, Inc.*

DEAN ACHESON

FRANK CANCELLARE, ACME

ROSTRUM CONFERENCE

ARTHUR E. SCOTT, INP

IN the photo at the left, Speaker Sam Rayburn confers with Rep. Charles A. Halleck of Indiana (*back to camera*) and House Minority Leader Joseph W. Martin, Jr. (*right*) of Massachusetts on the rostrum of the House of Representatives during a roll call.

More than eight months after the opening of the first session of the 82nd Congress there had been a great deal of speech-making, many conferences and very little actual legislation passed. Some of the reasons advanced for this slow pace were: the close scrutiny Congress was giving to the Administration's proposals; a hostile coalition of Republicans and Southern Democrats; the Administration's tardiness in presenting its greatly enlarged mobilization program.

On the list of unfinished business is Truman's "Fair Deal"—national health insurance, the Brannan plan, civil rights legislation and repeal of the Taft-Hartley Act.

With a presidential election coming up next year, the Democrats are sure to make political issues out of the record of the past session of Congress, and one of the strongest is likely to be price controls. With prices expected to rise under the amended Defense Production Act, which the President called the "worst" he has ever had to sign, it is obvious that the Republicans will be accused of having weakened anti-inflation controls.

In the field of international debate, the United Nations continued to accumulate a record file of the spoken word—in many fields and in many tongues. But actual accomplishments are not so well defined. After a year of "police action" in Korea a clear-cut victory has not been obtained yet the lesson of collective action against aggression is an important one. Red China has been branded as an "aggressor" in Korea but economic sanctions are not being enforced, and her chances of being admitted to the UN as the representative government of China are less good. At any rate, the United Nations still remains an important cog in the machinery of diplomatic relations.

ACTION AT THE UN (PAGES 274-5)

DAVID LINTON

Up until the peace talks at Kaesong, U. S. operations in Korea had reached big-war proportions. With a fighting front 7,000 miles away from home, more than 13 million tons of war supplies have been transported from the U. S. across the Pacific to Korea since June, 1950. In addition, an amount in excess of 70 million barrels of gasoline, oil and fuel for jet planes has been shipped to the war zone. *U. S. News & World Report* recently stated that "To support the shooting war for one month, hundreds of U. S. ships are carrying 1.4 million tons of ammunition, weapons, food, clothing, vehicles and equipment to Korea. Other fleets of tankers are now carrying 10 million barrels of fuel to Korea monthly. About 100,000 soldiers, airmen and civilians are being carried by ship to or from Korea each month."

Much of these supplies and men are moved by air into Korea from bases in Japan. Over 1,000 tons of supplies are averaged in daily flights. Nearly all evacuation of wounded is done by air, with over 125,000 evacuees flown out as of last June.

To carry on the battle in Korea; to man the supply lines; to build up and train an adequate defense force for western Europe and defense of the U. S.; to build up an industrial machine capable of equipping and supplying these forces, as well as a civilian population, and provide for stock-piling of critical materials, the U. S. has had to take a long look at its manpower. The Draft, volunteer enlistments, the calling up of Reserve (right) and National Guard units—all have been necessary to meet the emergency. But to achieve this proper balance it is imperative that civilian and military mobilization fall in step.

MARINE RESERVES

BOB DOTY, DAYTON JOURNAL-HERALD

"EXERCISE SWARMER"

H. L. GRIFFIN, WIDE WORLD

Part of the intensified training program for the military has been the extended use of the air-borne troops. Last year extensive field maneuvers were carried out under simulated battle conditions. "Exercise Swarmer" (*left*) at Camp McCall, North Carolina, tested both men and equipment in mass jumps.

TV ANTENNAS BROUGHT CRIME INTO THE LIVING ROOM

CRIME INVESTIGATORS

FOR a week and a half during the middle of March the Senate Crime Investigating Committee, under the chairmanship of Estes Kefauver (D.—Tenn.) held hearings in New York City. Before the Committee and across the screens of millions of television sets, passed a parade of thugs, gangsters, gamblers, racketeers, police, and small and big-time politicians. An estimated 20 million persons saw and heard the proceedings. Household chores went undone, meals uncooked, business unattended, stores were empty and even the stock market trading dropped, as a shocked and fascinated public watched the sordid tale of crime unfold before their

eyes. Into millions of living rooms stepped the shadowy figures of the underworld, the political fixers, heads of syndicates, the chiselers and swindlers to sweat and squirm, lie and evade, or refuse to answer the questions put to them by the Committee.

Most of the questioning was done by Rudolph Halley, chief counsel for the Committee, whose relentless questioning in a flat, metallic voice was brilliant and masterful.

Some of the major results of the hearings were: (1) Ambassador-to-Mexico O'Dwyer was contradicted, under oath, about the receipt of a $10,000 gift while Mayor, and his

SENATORS HUNT, WILEY, KEFAUVER, TOBEY AND O'CONOR OF THE SENATE CRIME IN

prosecution of Murder, Inc. as District Attorney, as well as his relations with Costello, James Moran, Sherman and other underworld figures were sharply questioned; (2) Three top underworld figures, Frank Costello, Joe Adonis and Frank Erickson were cited for contempt of Congress, and since then both Adonis and Erickson have received jail sentences; (3) Costello and five Anastasia brothers face possible separate investigations of their immigration records for possible deportation proceedings, and much of their undercover power in politics has been brought to light; (4) Brooklyn policy racketeer Louis Weber was arrested for perjury; (5) N. Y. C. Water Commissioner James J. Moran, given the $15,000 a year life-time post just before O'Dwyer quit as Mayor in 1950, and, accused of accepting $55,000 from a firemen's association, resigned his post on the demand of Mayor Impelliteri, and has been convicted of perjury, in

connection with his testimony regarding his contacts with Louis Weber, policy racketeer. Other witnesses to appear before the Committee, were Virginia Hill, intimate of most of the bigtime mobsters, who insisted she knew nothing of their finances, and whose income payments are now under investigation; John P. Crane, president of the Uniformed Firemen's Association, who testified that he had given O'Dwyer and Moran a total of $65,000 in gifts and campaign contributions; also several political bosses, racketeers, and waterfront organizers from New Jersey.

Throughout all of this testimony an unfamiliar voice rose in an almost forgotten type of oratory, full of Latin phrases, Biblical quotations, and the wrath of old-fashioned indignation. This was the voice of New Hampshire's Senator Tobey, who stirred memories of standards of conduct which almost seem to have gone out of style in government service today.

O'DWYER PONDERS A QUESTION

A DAPPER O'DWYER BECOMES QUITE RUFFLED (*right*)

COSTELLO BEFORE THE CRIME COMMITTEE ALFRED EISENSTADT, LIFE © *Time, Inc.*

COSTELLO, THE SUAVE BUSINESSMAN LEONARD McCOMBE, LIFE © *Time, Inc.*

JAMES J. MORAN MARTIN LEDERHANDLER, WW   **LOUIS WEBER** SAM SCHULMAN, INP

EDWARD J. FLORIO ANTHONY CAMERANO, WW   **JACOB GUZIK** WIDE WORLD

JOE ADONIS WIDE WORLD

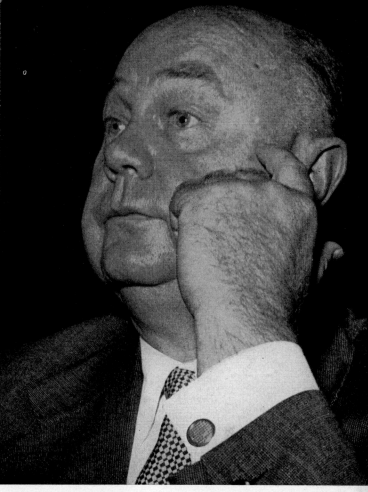

FRANK ERICKSON HERBERT K. WHITE, WW

ALBERT ANASTASIA ANTHONY CAMERANO, WW

VIRGINIA HILL INTERNATIONAL

MEDAL OF HONOR WINNERS

WIDE WORLD

Wearing the Nation's highest combat award for valor, the Medal of Honor, Capt. Harvey of Pasadena, Calif.; Capt. Lewis L. Millett of Haverhill, Mass.; M/Sgt. Stanley Adams of Olathe, Kansas; and Sgt. Einar Ingman of Tomahawk, Wisc., listen to President Truman speak on July 15 after presentation of the awards at the White House. In the rear are (*left to right*) Secy. of Air, Thomas Finletter; Army Chief of Staff, Gen. J. Lawton Collins; former Chief of Naval Operations, the late Adm. Forrest P. Sherman; Maj. Gen. N. F. Twining; Under Secy. of the Navy, Dan Kimball and Secy. of Defense, George C. Marshall.

HELL BOMB

By WILLIAM L. LAURENCE

EDITORS NOTE: These excerpts are from "The Hell Bomb", by William L. Laurence, famous Pulitzer Prize winner and science reporter for the N.Y. Times, published last year by Alfred A. Knopf, Inc. Copyright 1950 by The Curtis Publishing Co. and the author.

I FIRST heard about the hydrogen bomb in the spring of 1945 in Los Alamos, New Mexico, where our scientists were putting the finishing touches on the model-T uranium, or plutonium, fission bomb. I learned to my astonishment that, in addition to this work, they were already considering preliminary designs for a hydrogen-fusion bomb, which in their lighter moments they called the "Super-duper" or just the "Super."

I can still remember my shock and incredulity when I first heard about it from one of the scientists assigned to me by Dr. J. Robert Oppenheimer as guides in the Dantesque world that was Los Alamos, where the very atmosphere gave one the sense of being in the presence of the supernatural. It seemed so fantastic to talk of a superatomic bomb even before the uranium, or the plutonium, bomb had been completed and tested—in fact, even before anybody knew that it would work at all—that I was inclined at first to disbelieve it. Could anything be more powerful, I found myself thinking, than a weapon that, on paper at least, promised to release an explosive force of 20,000 tons of TNT?

So at the first opportunity I put the question to Professor Hans A. Bethe, of Cornell University, one of the world's top atomic scientists, who headed the elite circle of theoretical physicists at Los Alamos. Dr. Bethe, I knew, was the outstanding authority in the world qualified to talk about the subject, since he was the very man who first succeeded in explaining how the fusion of hydrogen in the sun is the source of energy that will make it possible for life to continue on earth for billions of years.

"Is it true about the superbomb?" I asked him. "Will it really be as much as fifty times as powerful as the uranium or plutonium bomb?"

I shall never forget the impact on me of his quiet answer as he looked away toward the Sangre de Cristo (Blood of Christ) mountain range, their peaks turning blood-red in the New Mexico twilight. "Yes," he said, "it could be made to equal a million tons of TNT." Then, after a pause: "Even more than a million."

The tops of the mountains seemed to catch fire as he spoke.

Oddly enough, the discovery of the principle that made the atomic bomb possible also brought with it the promise that a "deuterium (Continued on Page 390)

ATOMIC BLASTS IN NEVADA DESERT

D. SCHIEK, *Las Vegas Review Journal, via Acme*

(PAGE 291) AEC, *via Wide World*

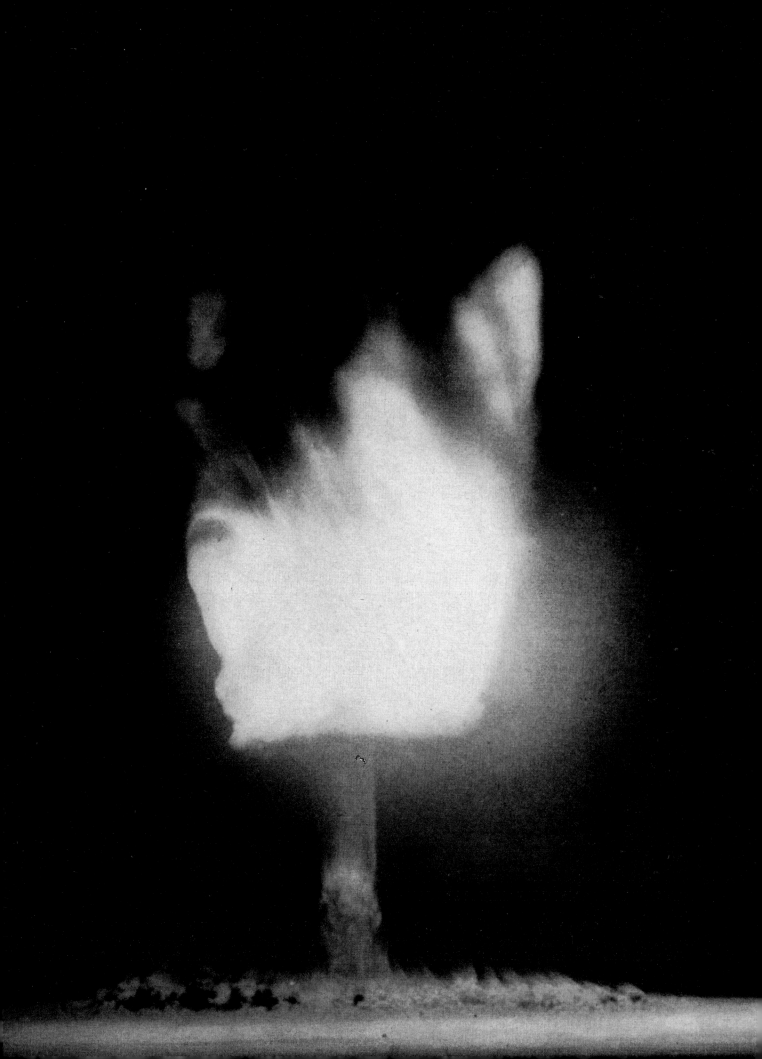

ATOMIC BLAST IN SOUTHERN NEVADA

To get the series (*above*) *Life* photographer J. R. Eyerman set up high-speed aerial cameras near Highway 95, about 35 miles southeast of the blast point. As the first of 4 blasts went off at 5.46 A.M. on Feb. 1, its flsh triggered a photo-electric cell which started the cameras. These had been stopped down to f/32 and set for 1/400th of a second. In

ATOMIC BLASTS AT ENIWETOK (PAGES 294-297)

J. R. EYERMAN, LIFE © *Time, Inc.*

the first photo (*top, left*) taken at .032 second after the explosion, a wide expanse has been lighted up. At .04 second (*center, left*) it has reached its greatest intensity, after which it dies down until by .09 second (*center, right*) only a light speck remains. Fifteen minutes later, only a wisp of smoke was visible over the hills as the dawn broke over Nevada.

ARMY-NAVY JOINT TASK FORCE (WIDE WORLD)

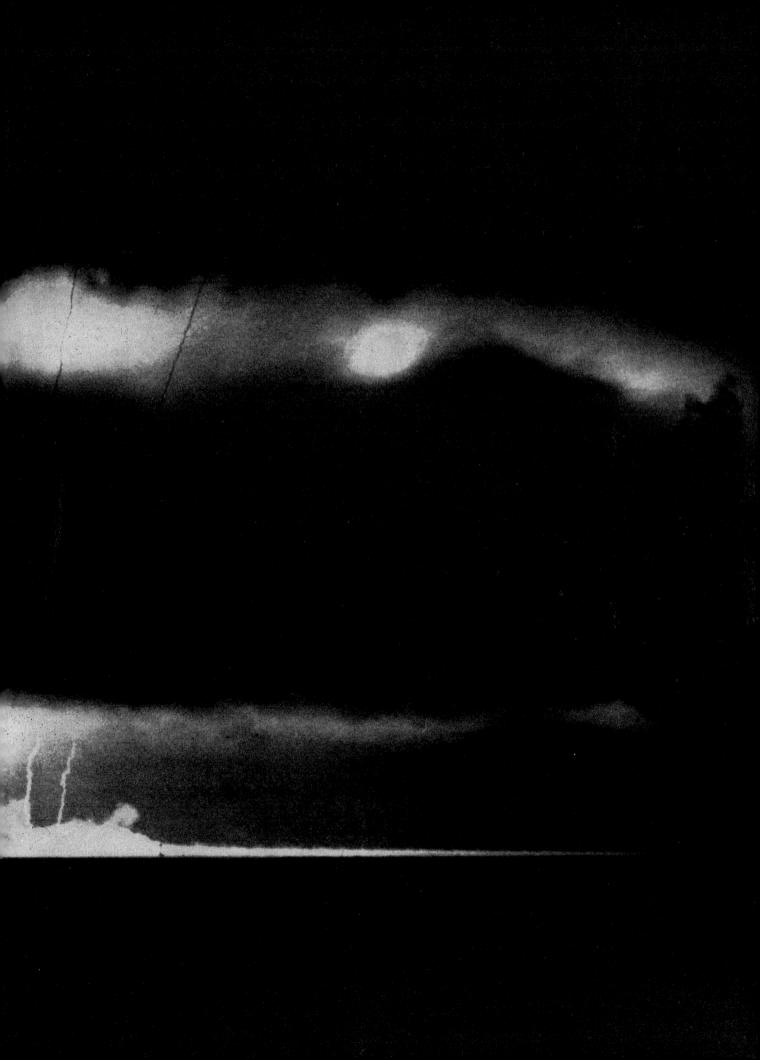

ATOM SPIES SOBELL AND MR. & MRS. ROSENBERG

M. ZIMMERMAN, WW

ALGER HISS, 46, is shown at left leaving Federal Court in New York to start serving a 5-year sentence for perjury. At his first trial the jury was unable to bring a verdict against him, but the second jury in a later trial found the evidence overwhelmingly against him and brought in a guilty verdict. Hiss tried to appeal his case, but the request was rejected by the Court.

Hiss had a bright career as a lawyer and later as an assistant Secretary in the State Dept. The charges made against him, stealing State Dept. secrets for the Russians, were the forerunners of similar charges brought against William Remington, former War Production Board employee and alleged Communist, who also received a 5-year sentence in jail which was appealed and the judgment reversed in August.

A Federal jury in New York found all three defendants in the nation's first Atom spy trial guilty of espionage in behalf of Russia during and after World War II. They are Julius Rosenberg, electrical engineer, his wife, Ethel, and Morton Sobell, electronics engineer. The jury deliberated over seven hours before they could bring in the verdict. All three had pleaded innocent to charges of transmitting key secrets to the Soviets about the Atom bomb. The Rosenbergs were sentenced to death by Federal Judge Irving Kaufman who said: "Plain, deliberate, contemplated murder is dwarfed in magnitude by comparison with the crime you have committed." Sobell was sentenced to 30 years. If the penalties are carried out, the Rosenbergs will be the first spies ever executed by order of a U. S. civil court.

ALGER HISS GOES TO JAIL

WIDE WORLD

JACOB MINDEL

MARION BACHRACH

ALEXANDER L. TRACHTENBERG

MEMBERS OF THE HIERARCHY (*Top and bottom row*)

AMTER & WIFE

ACME   BENJAMIN DAVIS & EUGENE DAVIS

ELIZABETH GURLEY FLYNN

CLAUDIA JONES

ISIDORE BEGUN

PETTIS PERRY

BETTY GANNETT

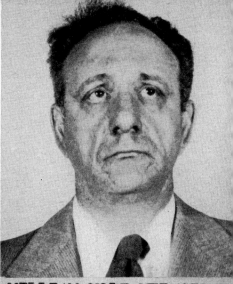

WILLIAM WOLF WEINSTONE

FREDERICK V. FIELD

SIMON W. GERSON

ALEXANDER BITTELMAN

VICTOR J. JEROME

PRESIDENT OF FRANCE PAYS A VISIT TO NEW YORK

A. B. RICKERBY, ACME

On March 28 French President Vincent Auriol arrived on the first formal visit ever paid the U. S. by a president of the Republic of France. During his Washington stay he ad-dressed the American Foreign Ministers on the unity of West Europe and the Western Hemisphere, and told a joint session of Congress that France was striving for a free Europe.

"WELL, I'LL BE DARNED!"

FRANCIS J. GRANDY, STARS AND STRIPES

On April 11, Truman announced that he had relieved Gen. Douglas MacArthur of all of his commands (UN, Allied and U. S.) in the Far East. The news pleased most of the UN nations, who feared an all-out war, and caused a violent split at home. Gen. Eisenhower's reaction is shown (above) as he received the news. (*Photo from Wide World.*)

MacArthur REVIEWS A PARADE IN N. Y.

A. B. RICKERBY, ACME

The recall of MacArthur stirred up a bitter controversy in the U. S. Public reaction was strong, articulate and immediate. Upon his arrival in the U. S., his first visit in 14 years, he was accorded a hero's welcome without parallel. Few questioned the President's right to dismiss the general but many objected to the shoddy manner in which it had been

MacARTHUR WELCOMED IN N. Y.

A. B. RICKERBY, ACME

done. An investigation was started by the Senate Armed Services and Foreign Relations Committee which lasted for 42 days and recorded 2,045,000 words of testimony from MacArthur, the Joints Chiefs of Staff and the Secretaries of Defense and State, as well as others connected with our foreign policies in the Far East during World War II.

O N April 28 the Hungarian government released Robert A. Vogeler after 17 months' imprisonment as a U. S. spy. Under a ransom deal negotiated by the State Department (which included: re-opening of Hungarian consulates here that had been closed in protest, the lifting of a U. S. ban on travel in Hungary, and return to Hungary of $70 million worth of property looted by the Nazis and held in Germany's U. S. zone), Vogeler was released to U. S. officials at the Hungarian-Austrian border, and was re-united in Vienna with his wife who had constantly spurred the U. S. State Department to work for his release.

Back in this country, Vogeler repudiated as rubbish, the confession which he had been forced to sign in a Budapest prison.

The Czech government announced on April 26 the arrest of William Oatis, AP's bureau chief in Prague, on a charge of actions hostile to the Czech government. He was accused of using his position to spy for the U. S., and sentenced to 10 years' imprisonment by a State Court in Prague on July 4. President Truman immediately denounced the imprisonment, and on July 17, a bill was introduced in Congress calling for retaliatory measures against Czechoslovakia unless Oatis is released.

Still a third iron-curtained kangaroo court decision found Hungarian Archbishop Joseph Groez guilty of crimes against the state, and sentenced him to 15 years in jail. Groez, who succeeded Cardinal Mindszenty, was prosecuted by Mindszenty's prosecutor.

ROBERT A. VOGELER

WIDE WORLD

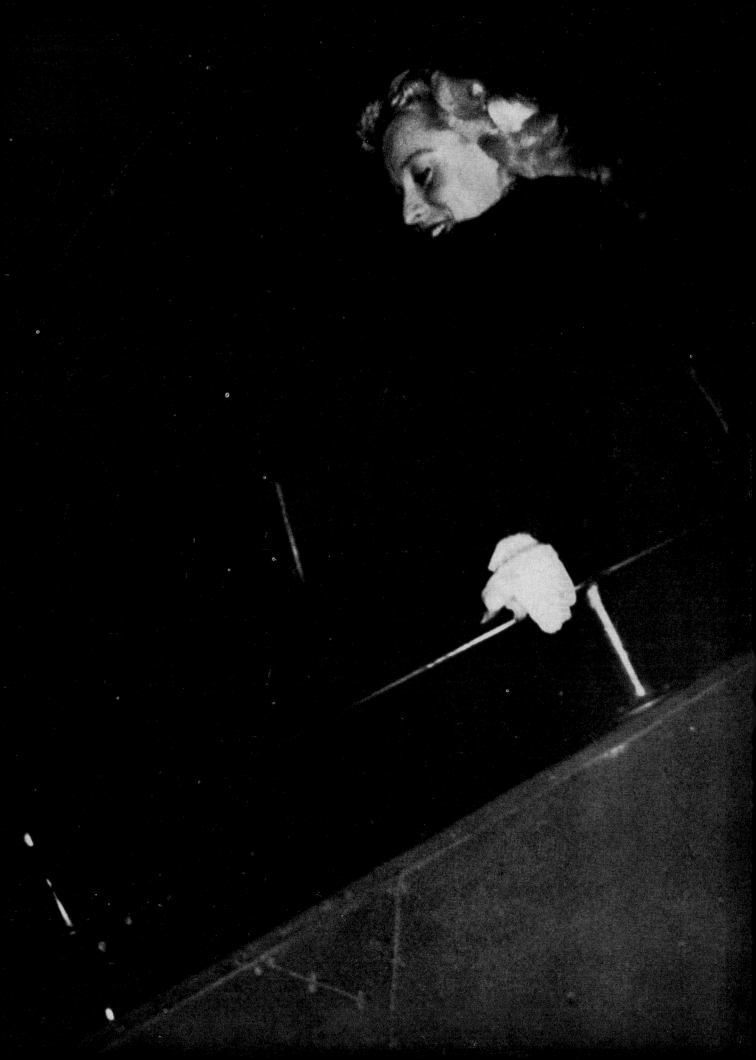

FAREWELLS

A. B. RICKERBY, ACME

At the end of May, 5,000 men of the U. S. Army 4th Division embarked in New York for service in Germany as reinforcement of U. S. land forces in western Europe got under way. Here are scenes at the dock as the troops bid farewell.

JOHN FOSTER DULLES

THE end, or a new beginning? The question of a final peace with Japan in the six years since the end of fighting has been overshadowed by the greater menace to Germany, and by the problems of dealing with Communism here and abroad. Finally, however, the peace seemed at hand. Largely put together by John Foster Dulles, the basic terms of the treaty, unashamedly pushed through by Washington, provide for Japan's right of self-defense as a sovereign power, the withdrawal of occupation troops within 90 days of the signing (though agreements may be made for the stationing of troops in Japan), the reduction of the nation to her four home islands, and reparations to be paid in the form of manufactured goods (but many countries want cash—which the U.S. would probably have to provide).

With an informal attitude unusual in such high-powered negotiations, changes were discussed in diplomatic conference; no formal peace conference was held at all. Invitations to the ceremonies of signing the treaty were sent to some thirty nations, with the conference to be held in San Francisco (after the date of this writing) beginning Sept. 4, 1951.

At the last minute, Russia and Poland accepted, apparently for the purpose of throwing monkey wrenches. They would hardly like the treaty, but it appeared that England, Australia, the Philippines and many smaller countries did not think much of it either. The Pacific nations' fears were obvious: in our build-up of Japan's industrial strength, would we be handing her a beautifully-worded invitation to "try again" in the Pacific? Then too, they said: China was not to be represented, because no one can decide which government should represent China—thus presumably leaving the way open for Japan to sign a separate treaty with whichever government appears to be winning at some later date.

Japan forms one of our barriers against the spread of Communism; we must bolster her up whether we like it or not. But—it is inconceivable that the whole mentality of a people may be changed in less than a decade, and we only fool ourselves if we think that a full dose of democracy has rubbed off onto the Japanese people in the short time of our occupation. Our hope is that they fear Communism enough to throw in their hand permanently with the Western nations.

ERIC DRAKE, GENERAL MANAGER OF ANGLO-IRANIAN

E. WORTH, WW

The senseless inevitability of the oil talks represented both another nail in Britain's Imperialist coffin, and an indication of fanatical, irresponsible nationalism on Iran's part. But—meeting after meeting about the future of Anglo-Iranian came to naught, despite the efforts of President Truman's personal peace-maker, W. Averell Harriman. Late in August, negotiations were broken off by Iran's refusal of Britain's best bid. The next move in the Middle East may be up to Russia.

ASSAULT BOAT HITS UNDERWATER DEMOLITION CHARGE

The summer of 1951 produced some of the largest and most arduous training exercises since the war. Large units of ground troops were used combined with close tactical air support. Particular emphasis was placed on the use of airborne troops and development of the technique of air-drop of heavy equipment. The training was realistic and rough

DAVID GLEASON, U. S. ARMY

and there were casualties. The dramatic photo (*above*) shows men and equipment being hurled skyward as an assault boat of the 47th Infantry Division at Camp Rucker, Ala. accidently hit an underwater demolition charge which had drifted into its path. Ten men were injured, one (*at top of picture*) sustained a broken back, but no one was killed.

THE PRICE WAR

A. B. RICKERBY, ACME

O<small>N</small> May 29th Macy's quietly cut the price of over 5,000 articles of merchandise by 6%. The price war was on. Competitors quickly slashed their prices to keep pace with Macy's. People, like the women at left, went scurrying to stores to pick up items before they were sold out or the original retail price was restored. Mixmasters, vacuum-cleaners, pots and pans and just about everything but clothing made for a shopper's heaven, if the shopper had the strength to fight the crowds. The entire war came as reaction to the new price controls imposed by the Office of Price Stabilization.

Last November, with prices steadily rising, the Government felt it was time to step in and put a curb on the nation's economy. President Truman picked the Mayor of Toledo, wisecracking, likable Mike DiSalle (*right*) to head the OPS. His first step was to put an immediate 30-day price freeze on everything so that the OPS could study the situation. Here was a beginning and DiSalle put it this way: "The trouble around here is that everbody is so afraid of making a mistake that nobody gets anything done. We are bound to make some mistakes." His goal is not to bring prices back to their 1946 level. He just wants to control prices to prevent them from going sky-high. The biggest stumbling block confronting DiSalle is the wage-earnings policy that must be settled before prices can be checked. He is working on this problem now. DiSalle likes to work and he's a fighter. A confirmed optimist, Mike DiSalle plans to have prices where he wants them by fall.

MIKE DiSALLE

W J. SMITH, WIDE WORLD

RED DELEGATES AT KAESONG

GEORGE E. SWEERS, WIDE WORLD

"Korea is the most acute problem today. The Soviet peoples believe that a peaceful settlement can be achieved there. As a first step, discussions should be started between the belligerents for a cease-fire and an armistice providing for the mutual withdrawal of forces from the 38th parallel." With these words in a 15-minute recorded broadcast from N.Y. Soviet Deputy Foreign Minister Jacob Malik gave the signal for peace talks in Korea. With UN forces in good tactical positions (in most cases north of the parallel) after having repulsed the Reds' major spring offensive, it seemed evident that the war in Korea was becoming too costly, the Communists were getting ready to attack in some other part of the world, or a breather was needed to build up for a new offensive in Korea.

With Kaesong as the accepted conference point, negotia-

tions were started by the appointed delegates on July 10. Vice Adm. Charles Turner Joy led the UN delegation of two U. S. and one South Korean officers, while Gen. Nam Il and one North Korean and two Chinese officers represented the Reds. After more than a month of meetings (with two interruptions when Gen. Ridgway threatened to end the talks because of truce violations) both sides were still deadlocked over the agenda, and on Aug. 16 Adm. Joy suggested that the matter be turned over to a small subcommittee from both sides, hoping that an informal atmosphere might effect a compromise. For obviously political reasons the Reds were adamant concerning a buffer line at the 38th. The UN delegation was equally firm about rejecting the 38th on the grounds that it was an indefensible line, but were willing to discuss a line that would approximate the present battle lines.

GEN. RIDGWAY & ADM. JOY

GEORGE E. SWEERS, WIDE WORLD

NEWS HIGHLIGHTS

As in other years, highlights of the news were made by many people in all walks of life. Left to right (*photo credits in parenthesis*) top row: On Nov. 22, 1950, a L. I. railroad collision took the lives of 78 persons and injured 300 (*Russell Larson, International*). In Pittsburgh, Pa. Joe Walcott won the heavyweight championship by knocking out Ezzard Charles in the 7th round on July 18, 1951, (*Walter Stein, Wide World*). Middle row: Franco's Spain was being considered for a role in the Atlantic Defense set-up (*INP*). Ernest Bevin, 70, Britain's Foreign Secretary, 1945-51, died in London on April 14, 1951, (*INP*). King Gustav V, 92, of Sweden died in Stockholm Oct. 29, 1950 after reigning nearly 43 years (*INP*). On Sept. 22, 1950, Dr. Ralph Bunche was awarded the 1950 Nobel Peace Prize for his work as a UN mediator, in ending the war in Palestine (*INP*). Peron tightened his dictatorial rule of Argentina by closing one of his last and strongest critics, *La Prensa* newspaper (*INP*). Al Jolsen, famous stage, screen and radio singer died in San Francisco

on Oct. 23, 1950, at the age of 67 (*INP*). Bottom row: In April John Foster Dulles, veteran Republican Foreign Policy expert, accepted the invitation of Pres. Truman and Dean Acheson to serve as advisor to the State Department (*Frank Mastro, INP*). Louis Johnson, controversial Secretary of Defense resigned on Sept. 19, 1950, and Pres. Truman appointed Gen. George C. Marshall to succeed him (*Charles Corte, Acme*). On Aug. 19, 1951 Bernard Baruch, "elder statesman" and advisor to presidents quietly celebrated his 81st birthday in New York (*Maria Martel, Flair Magazine*). Defying the party machines, Vincent Impellitteri, independent candidate for Mayor of New York, scored a sweeping victory at the polls on Nov. 7, 1950 (*Hans Reinhart, INP*). Herbert Hoover, former President of the United States, started "the great debate" on the subject of defense when he stated in a radio address that America's defense lines should be the Atlantic and Pacific Oceans, not the continents of Europe and Asia. (*Herbie Scharfman, INP*). On Jan. 19, 1951 Pres. Truman appointed Eric Johnston, President of the Motion Picture Association, to the job of Economic Stabilization Administrator replacing Alan Valentine. His job was to formulate control policies regulating wages, prices, rents, profits, credit and rationing (*Henry Burroughs, WW*).

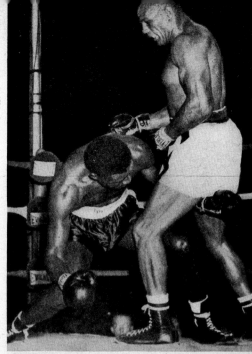

FOR DEMOCRACY

AMERICA

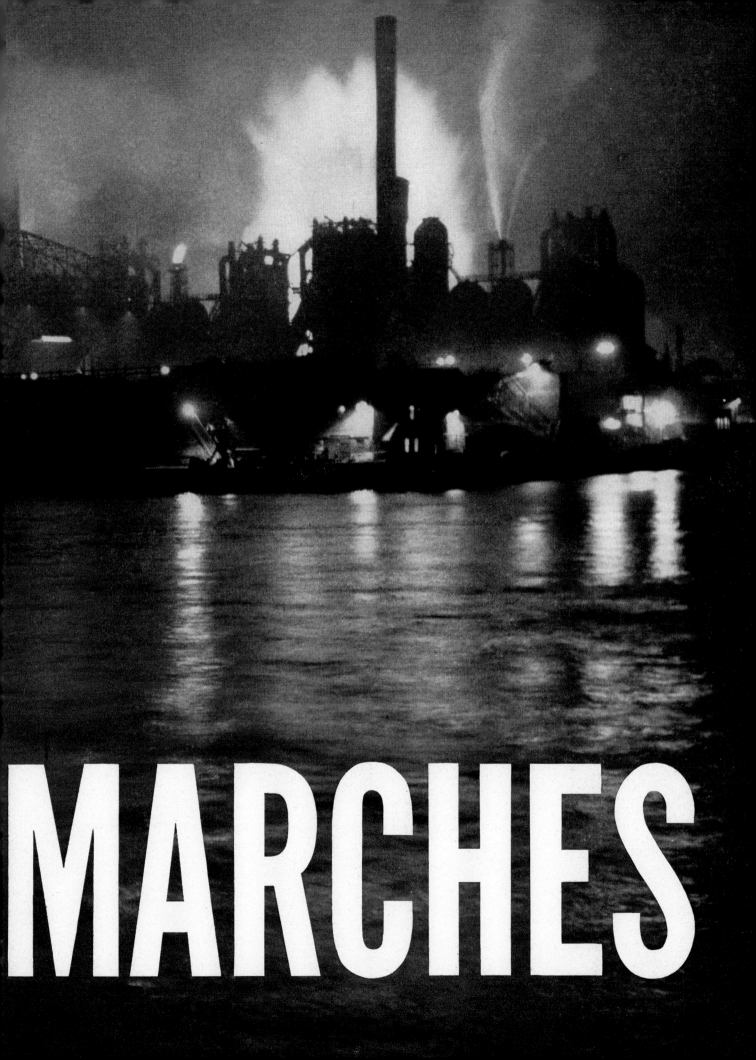

MARCHES

WORK

PLAN

Brains and blueprints—first step to produce economic base and capacity to mobilize.

The present mobilization program of the United States has the dual aim of simultaneously developing a growth in military power and an expansion of the basic economic strength which supports and underlies military strength. With the Armed Forces the "cutting edge" of the military machine, the over-all, long-range fighting strength of the nation rests on the broad base of its ability to produce new weapons, its supplies of raw materials, its capacity to transport materials and people, and its ability to feed and sustain its population, today, tomorrow and perhaps for fifty years. This must be planned, coordinated and executed in a shifting atmosphere of war and peace.

At the head of and directing this enormous master plan is Charles E. Wilson, working symbol of the American production man. Under his hard-fisted direction, as chief of the Office of Defense Mobilization, the blueprints have been drawn and the vast machinery is slowly meshing into gear. But not without friction—the friction of rising prices, increased taxes, wage freezes, farm subsidies, allocations of scarce materials, man-power demands, both civilian and military, increased aid to Europe and Asia, the Korean war, and an up-coming presidential election next year.

DRAFTING ROOM   WESTINGHOUSE

TEST

Atomic weapons or easier-opening buttons, research and testing show up in the payoff.

Not one single piece of military equipment, machinery or production instruments are put into mobilization work without exhaustive testing. Thousands of dollars may be spent on a model—hand-made in many cases—of a plane, electronic gadget, instrument or gun before it is put into assembly-line production. Flight tests of airplanes are a familiar, romantic routine to most Americans. Far less familiar are such tests as those conducted in cold rooms, as shown here, or under conditions simulating the desert's dry heat—in nearly-complete vacuums or under the pressure of many atmospheres; these tests go on day and night unknown for the most part, a vital link in our mobilization effort.

Even that airplane test flight is no longer movie-thriller material. A pilot, pad and pencil were the only necessary things for testing Boeing's PW-9 in 1923. "Strut vibrates: beef it up . . . Not enuf rudder control: make it bigger," wrote Boeing's test pilot then. Today, the test-flight program for Boeing's jet bomber, XB-47, has taken 22 months and hundreds of men to test; two models of this plane, built, tested and delivered, cost nearly $12,000,000.

Research, electronics, atomic energy—these are the magic words of today—and every phase of our country's scientific development is used in the testing of material. Nor is the testing finished when a product is delivered. Then, men of the Armed Forces take over. What is it like in combat? Can we have more speed? More versatility? More power? These are the tests that count.

Across the sandy hills of Nevada last winter rolled the glare and thunder of new atomic weapons' tests. What they were, no one would say. But these tests, spectacular as they were, should not outshine more routine tasks, when the payoff is in battle.

COLD TEST

ROBERT HICE, *Westinghouse*

MOVE

Materials, arms, food must span continents and oceans, by air, ship, rail and motor.

We learned, during the heart-breaking days in World War II when Nazi submarine wolf packs sank ships at will out of Allied convoys, that the best material in the world is no good at the factories. Transportation, a staggering mobilization problem, must be kept ahead of potential losses and potential production capacity, to move raw materials, food, workers, military equipment, soldiers—transportation by truck, by rail, sea and air—to the far corners of the globe.

In ten years, the trucks operating in the U. S. have grown from 4,590,000 to more than 8,200,000—with a present tonnage hauled, of 115 billion ton-miles a year. Truckers, running on express schedules and on short hauls where rail transport would be too costly or impractical, have shown that they can do the job.

Defense Mobilization Chief Wilson, in his second quarterly report to the President, released these figures; a goal, for mid-1953 of 1,850,000 freight railroad cars in operation by Class I roads. But use, performance of the cars, has and will continue to, improve. During 1951's first quarter, net ton-miles per freight-car-day averaged 940, compared to an average of 770 for 1949 and 1950. New facilities, new equipment, are being built by the roads, to face a stern test.

Shipping is in comparatively healthy state, and growing apace. During the quarter covered in Wilson's report, 500,000 tons of equipment were shipped under the Mutual Defense Assistance Program alone, to free nations.

Air transport, largely used for perishable consumer goods, has been developed for defense mobilization primarily by the Air Force. New planes, new techniques and brave flying crews have already made history in the evacuation of wounded from Korea.

ORE CARS

E. BUBLEY, *Standard Oil Co. (N. J.)*

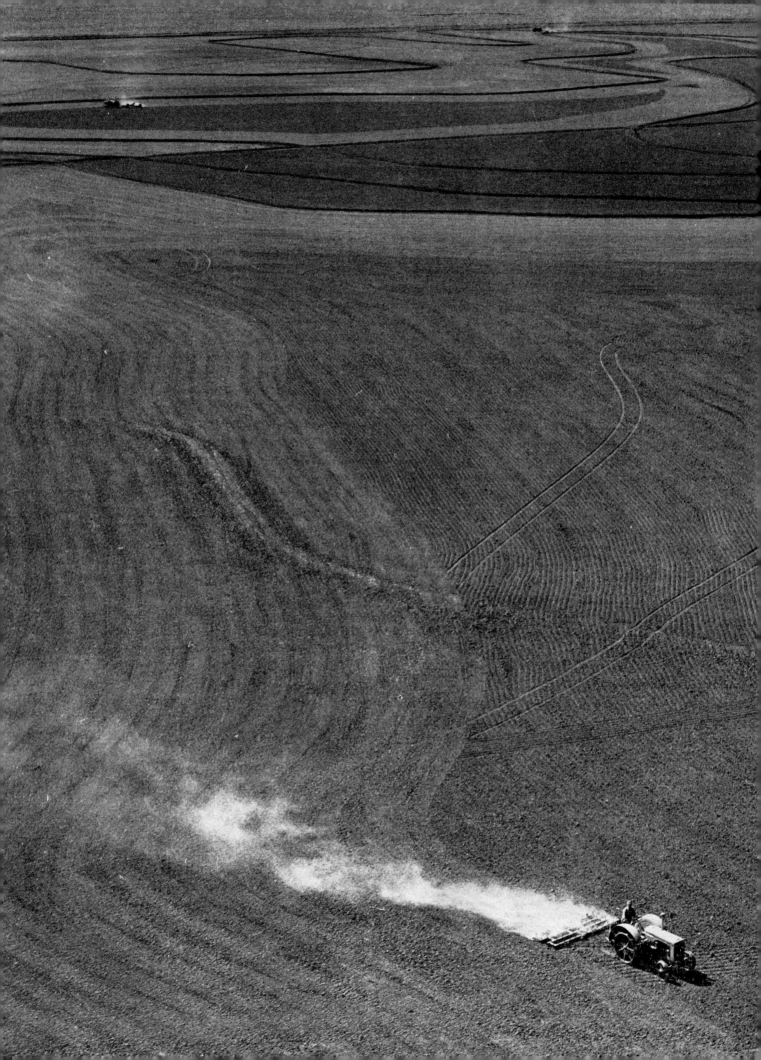

PLANT

With maximum cultivation, U.S. must produce raw materials for national defense.

The importance of the farmer's role in mobilization cannot possibly be under-estimated. Beside the necessary food supplies, much of the basic material for manufactured goods, clothing, lumber—come from the land. To promote a gain in food production would be to curtail some other part of the program, for nearly all arable land in the U.S. is now under cultivation.

The goal for American farmers, production 4% above 1950's record, is well on the way, despite serious obstacles. Among these obstacles are the year's terrible floods, droughts, and bad growing weather, as well as shortages. Some machinery, sulphur and chlorine for DDT and 2,4-D are in short supply already, as are fencing wire, baling wire and twine, and burlap bag stocks. The sulphur and nitrogen shortages seriously hampered production of commercial fertilizers for farm use.

Greater plantings were encouraged in such non-food crops as cotton, soybeans and grain sorghums. The call for 16 million bales of cotton in particular, resulted in lower acreages of corn in the cotton areas, and the ODM campaign in the Midwest emphasized greater plantings of feed crops to make up for the cut-backs in the South. This and other shifts in the balance of farm production have necessitated unceasing work on the part of national, state and local agricultural mobilization committees—for the most part literal "unsung heros".

Education of farmers is vital in order to preserve our soil capacity for future years. Thus, a farmer told to produce more per acre than ever before, shown how to plant to do it—must also be advised against plowing up and planting fields that ought to remain in grassland. The farmers too, are producing more with what they have.

RICE FARMING   ROBERT L. BROWNING

FEED

Army of workers and soldiers must be fed from land now producing record crops.

Greater—and always greater—yields is the goal and secret of mobilization on the nation's farms. With an army of workers, an army of soldiers and other parts of a free but hungry world to feed, the job is a far bigger one than we have ever faced before.

A record production is seen for this year —4% above last year's output—yet the total acreage planted in thirteen major food crops is about the same as last year. The percentage figures do not tell the whole story either, for 1951 weather was extremely unkind to the farmer.

Beside crop production, the expected output of meat and milk will also be increased. The fisheries industry has been maintained at a high level, as have fruit and vegetable packs in the canning industry. Thus the food supply of the United States assures a greater per-person consumption than last year.

In addition to the 1951 program, the ODM and the Department of Agriculture have long since been planning the 1952 production guides. State colleges, experiment stations and other government agencies are working on the problems with the farmers, in an effort to push the per-acre yields even higher. This effort, a result of planned growing programs, scientific progress and farmer education, is believed to be the hope of our food problems, for we already have under cultivation just about all of the land that can be economically worked.

Through a storm of public and congressional debate on food prices, profits and "worth-its-weight-in-gold hamburger", the farmer has kept his mouth shut and doggedly stayed on the job. The time to relax and talk, he believes, is when the harvest is in. In his case, it is a harvest in both the literal and the figurative sense of the word.

KANSAS WHEAT   MIKE SHEA

MAKE

Men, machines and industrial know-how are forging tools and arms for defense.

Military power is much more than weapons of war and men in uniform. It is also the power to produce—to produce more powerful and effective machines than our potential enemies, to produce more of them, and to produce them faster. This in turn depends upon the strength of the whole basic economy in all of its interrelated segments. For, the smallest machine-shop as well as a giant complex like General Motors, are linked up, directly or indirectly in defense mobilization, through allocation of critical materials and manpower, skilled and unskilled; defense contracts; subcontracts; activation of reserve plants, retooling; and setting of production goals.

Evidence of America's ability to "make" is to be found in a few production figures released by the Office of Defense Mobilization in its Quarterly Report of July 1, 1951.

"During the April-June quarter, about $10 billion of orders for military supplies, equipment and facilities were placed with industry. This brings to $42 billion the total of orders which have been placed since the Korean invasion, or were on the books, undelivered at the time. Of this amount, close to $10 billion has been delivered to date.

"Deliveries of end-items and construction activity have now reached a level of $1.5 billion monthly, compared to less than half a billion monthly pre-Korea.

"In aircraft, deliveries are currently about two-thirds higher than a year ago . . . production workers in the aircraft and parts industry increased from 185,000 a year ago to more than 300,000 in May 1951."

Concurrent with the military production program is a companion program to expand the Nation's capacity to produce, a program which, barring all-out war, will enable us to make ploughshares as well as guns.

FLAME TREATMENT

ROBERT HICE, *Westinghouse*

335

FUEL

With foreign oil shortages, U. S. coal, gas and oil producers set production records.

With greater uses of fuel for military, civilian and industrial consumers than has ever faced the world's reserves, the year saw also a greater threat than has faced the entire mobilization program. This was the loss, to the West, of vital oil from the Iranian fields—an output of 600,000 barrels per day. In typical American fashion, the sometimes-warring U.S. oil companies got together and announced an unprecedented step: an international pool which would, by the use of each other's pipelines, tankers and storage tanks, eliminate much wasteful duplication. The goal of this pool: savings up to half the lost Iranian production.

The United States is, according to Wilson, dependent upon foreign sources for nearly a million barrels of oil a day; Western European countries rely on imports for nearly all of their oil. In order to increase our own reserves, a goal of 43,400 new wells was set for 1951; the rate of wildcat drilling has risen 25% above 1950 and oil and gas producers' drilling operations are far above 1950 levels. An additional refinery capacity of 1 million barrels per day as a goal, is well under way. Special refining facilities have also grown, and the output of high-octane aviation gasoline is 55% above the level of last year.

Nowhere in the entire mobilization program, have the additional requirements been met by private industry as well as in the huge American oil companies. Coal producers, also vital in industrial mobilization, have for years been more beset by labor difficulties than have the oil companies. This year, the hope is that crippling strikes in the coal fields can be avoided, on a basis of critical national necessity, so that production of hard and soft coal will also meet new records for defense.

OIL REFINERY

MFL COSTON, *Humble Oil & Refining Co.*

ARM

Preparedness means a full arsenal of everything from tin cans to hydrogen bombs.

The military production program is highly selective in character. It is heavily concentrated in those items in which obsolescence has taken the largest toll on our World War II surplus stocks—and is therefore particularly heavy in aircraft, combat vehicles, and electronic equipment. The program also emphasizes new weapons, such as guided missles, and items for which long periods of time are required to organize production and subcontract for component parts. These include jet planes—fighters and long-range bombers—medium and heavy tanks, and of course the Atomic Energy program. But they also include the thousands of small items which make a fighting man more deadly on the battlefield in the air and on the sea. These include better combat rations, lighter weapons with greater power such as the bazooka, the recoilless rifles, improved firing devices, and electronic computors. The lessons learned in Korea have been costly but invaluable and have demonstrated the superiority of well-trained, well-armed troops over numerically superior but less well-equipped forces. Our tanks have outmatched the Russian T-34, and improved models are coming off the assembly lines, as well as a new heavy tank. Our air has not really been tested, to date our jets have a slight edge over the Russian MIG 15, but the overall stragedy of close tactical support as well as strategic bombing has been reemphasized.

The lesson of amphibious and airborne operations learned in World War II have not been forgotten either. Assault vehicles, from submersive jeeps to transport planes capable of carrying a light tank or 222 paratroopers have not only been developed but are on a production-line basis. The cost of preparedness is high but the eventual cost of unpreparedness is prohibitive.

UNDERWATER TESTS

WILLYS OVERLAND

PLANES

Better planes are coming off U.S. production lines.

Air power has increased enormously in importance, even since the blitz-to-atom-bomb days of World War II—and the United States is engaged in a titanic struggle with Russia in plane building. But our plane crews, it is believed are without exception far superior. How these planes and crews

will be used is a major problem. New bases are being built around the globe, and air transport (the only way to supply these far-flung bases with speedy supplies of fuel and weapons in the event of all-out war) is being constantly developed to keep pace.

The Air Force and the Navy Air Force are using valuable lessons learned in Korea in tactical training and use of planes. The Strategic Air Command sends almost nightly practice raids of mammoth B-36's and the now-medium B-29's across seas and continents.

With probably a slight lead in that race for planes, we must hold on to the leadership that we have in men and weapons, and plan even more powerful aircraft for them. For the future: the XC-99, a B-36 in transport dress, flying 150 tons 8,100 miles; XF-91 high-altitude jet interceptor; and the all-jet XB-52 (still more than a year from quantity production) heavy bomber.

SHIPS

Seaborne artillery and floating air dromes form backbone of U.S. defense orbit.

O ut of the welter of inter-service rivalry occasioned by the unification of the Armed Forces, has come a clearer definition of the Navy's future role. The Korean war has helped to bring this into sharper focus. At present the Navy is revamping its World War II equipment, while planning a new fleet to be centered about giant floating bases, equipped to handle A-bombers and jet fighters. In shipyards throughout the nation, ships from the "moth-ball" fleet are being refitted and recommissioned, including submarines being equipped with "snorkels."

The proposed "transition" fleet will ultimately include 14 carriers; 4 battleships; 5 converted cruiser carriers; 10 small carriers; 15 cruisers; 259 destroyers and destroyer escorts; 90 submarines; 685 patrol and other vessels.

The first of a new series of antisubmarine submarines has been launched, and a new compact radial-type diesel engine developed; a new rocket launcher has been perfected for aerial attack against submarines; and a ship-to-shore cableway has been produced, capable of carrying 30 tons an hour from a ship 500 feet offshore.

The Navy's first 60,000-ton aircraft carrier will come off the ways in 1955. Its main features will be a length of 1,040 feet, a crew of 3,500, 260,000 horsepower engines and will cost over $228 million.

While the hard core of the new Navy is being hammered into shape in the shipyards and training centers, U. S. battle fleets are guarding the Nation's shores and far-flung bases; fighting in Korea; and, in case of war, must be ready to sweep the sea lanes clear for inter-continental supply and provide a mobile platform from which the enemy's homeland can be brought under attack.

CARRIER LOADING AT NIGHT

RALPH CRANE, *Life* © *Time, Inc.*

MISSILES

With equations and slide-rules Science has pierced the boundaries of the impossible.

Over desert sands, in restricted areas of the oceans, and in the upper reaches of the stratosphere, scientists, engineers and military men are creating the missles of tomorrow —prototypes of the legendary "pushbutton warfare" of tomorrow.

During the five years preceding the Korean outbreak, the military research and development budget, exclusive of atomic energy, averaged $500 million annually. In the past year this budget has been doubled.

Because of the postwar research and development since 1945, we are reaching the production stage on a great many new and improved weapons and techniques.

The theory of guided missles, first put into combat use by the Germans in World War II, is being expanded to make it a vital weapon for defense.

Beyond the research stage are electronically-controlled and radar-guided missles which can be launched from land, or sea or air, against moving or stationary targets, as in the photo on the right. Here a U. S. Navy Martin Viking rocket is shown at the moment of launching from the deck of the U. S. S. Norton Sound, somewhere near the equator.

The most striking advances have been the field of atomic weapons. Atomic bombs, considerably improved over those used in World War II, are being produced on an industrial basis. The development of atomic warheads for artillery shells and guided missiles is proceeding, as is that of the atomic-powered submarine. Development of the Hydrogen bomb has gone beyond the stage of mere possibility, and in addition, progress is being made in defensive measures against atomic attacks, in methods of detecting and measuring radiation and in decontamination procedures.

To insure a continuation of this program the scientific manpower resources of the nation must be mobilized, carefully and selectively, and the training and ability of scientists used to maximum advantage.

MARTIN VIKING ROCKET   **U.S. NAVY**

LEAD

A time of crisis is producing men of vision, courage and leadership to mobilize the Nation for defense.

Heading up the Office of Defense Mobilization is Charles E. Wilson, who retired as president of the General Electric Co. to take on the job, and who during World War II had served brilliantly as head of the War Production Board. He is faced with the fantastic task of creating a production line capable of maintaining an army in combat in Korea, of supplying a defense army in western Europe as well as supporting its tottering economies, of equipping armed forces at home, and at the same time supplying as many peacetime civilian needs as possible.

For the defense of western Europe, Gen. Dwight D. Eisenhower has been called back to active duty from the presidency of Columbia University. Under his capable leadership and administrative ability member nations of the Atlantic Treaty Pact are being organized into a coordinated, defensive force against the danger of armed aggres-

sion from the East. Again the task is almost superhuman for it involves delicate international relations, distinct national problems which are political as well as economic. It is Eisenhower's job to weld the fragments into a mobile defense force capable of holding the first assault.

In the Far East a relatively unknown general is quietly and competently filling a vacant spot. This is General Matthew B. Ridgway, who took over command of the 8th Army after the death of Gen. Walker, and who, upon the relief from all commands of Gen. MacArthur, assumed overall command in the Far East. His tactical and administrative ability has been demonstrated in his handling of the Korean war and his greater role as administrator and negotiator at the peace talks current in Kaesong at this writing leaves little to be desired in the way of command decision. In times of crisis American leadership is being forged.

EISENHOWER   B. G. HOERTEL, *N. Y. Times*   •   WILSON   KARSH   •   RIDGWAY   HORACE BRISTOL

TRAIN

Men must be trained to use intricate weapons of warfare.

The Armed Forces are soon approaching the current goal of approximately 3.5 million—more than double the 1.5 million in uniform at the time of Korea.

During the past year voluntary enlistments accounted for more than half of all recruits drawn from civilian life (exclusive of reservists or National Guard units). These enlistments were primary considerations in the reduction of Selective Service calls from 80,000 in January, February, and March to 20,000 in June, 15,000 in July and 22,000 in August. On June 19 a comprehensive revision of the Selective Service Act lowered the draft age and increased the length of service. With heavy military and civilian demands manpower, a nation's most valuable asset, must be carefully and wisely selected and used.

AIRBORNE TRAINING

J. DOMINIS, *Life* © *Time, Inc.*

FIGHT

With men, arms and courage, America must be ready to meet aggression anywhere.

The decision to resist aggression in Korea was a moral one, made at a time when the Nation was completely unprepared for such a commitment. With great courage and at great cost our determination has been proven.

While negotiations seem to point toward an eventual cease-fire in Korea, the United States is continuing to build up its Army, Navy and Air Force. The quick demobilization in 1946 left the U.S. wholly unprepared for war in 1950. The small force of American troops, numbering less than 1½ million men was scattered in Europe and the Pacific. In the United States only one division (the 82nd Airborne) was trained and ready to fight. The Navy had mothballed the Fleet and the Air Force had stored 60,000 planes, most of them obsolete.

Congress passed a new Draft law and calls for 80,000 men a month came from the Army. Speed was the main objective and Reservists were called to duty to train the recruits. President Truman and Defense Secretary Marshall set a goal of 3½ million men in the Army by 1952. The Navy planned to build 173 new ships by 1953, and the Air Force was to increase its proposed 85 air groups to 105.

Not all of the men and arms were to go to Korea. A large part was to be sent to Europe to aid the starting of an army for the defense of Europe, headed by Supreme Commander Gen. Eisenhower. The Western powers seemed more in danger from Communism in Europe than the Far East. With Iran a tension spot in the Middle East, the Navy shifted many of its ships from Korea to form a larger Mediterranean fleet. Several bomber and fighter groups have already been transferred from the U. S. Air Force to SHAPE Air Wing.

GI IN KOREA

D. D. DUNCAN, *Life © Time, Inc.*
(From "This Is War" by D. D. Duncan)

PHOTO

In mobilization, photography is the universal tool assuring higher production and quality.

WITHOUT photography the mobilization effort would fail miserably! At every level of preparedness, photography—its varied processes and applications—is an invaluable tool. Functional photography is the newest basic method for all business and industry, presenting endless opportunities for savings both in time and money. It is to photography that the exceptionally high levels of production attained, in the defense effort of World War II and today's rapidly snowballing mobilization buildup, can be largely attributed.

The unique characteristics of photography enable it to do old tasks better, quicker and more easily—as well as accomplish new ones not before possible. Functional photography is accurate. It substitutes fact for theory, proof for faith. It is fast and lasting. Facts can be collected faster than the wink of an eye and yet remain unchanged through constant use. It provides an enduring account of conditions at the desired precise instant with no possibility of erroneous readings of transient variables. (*Continued on Page 356*)

WEAPON OF near future will be developed from test flights of rockets like this one at White Sands, N. M. Cameras in the rocket and on ground provide scientists with research data otherwise unobtainable. *U.S. Army Photograph.*

PHOTOGRAPHS like the one below help ordnance engineers perfect equipment. Invisible secrets in flight of artillery projectile (unsharp dark image), are clearly defined in this spark photograph from *PIO, Aberdeen Proving Ground.*

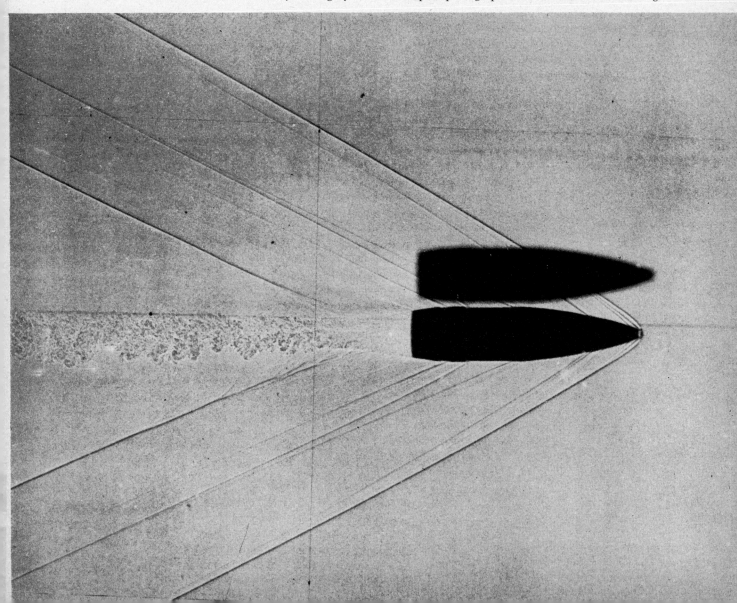

WHEN SENSITIVE instruments cannot do the job, photography does the work of evaluating the unseen. In rocket research, photographs like these provide otherwise impossible-to-obtain data. Above: An 11.75″ aircraft rocket was pictured by the Bowen Ribbon-Frame Camera as it penetrated a steel target and exploded behind it. Below: A fiery tail end view of sixteen rockets fired from a plane in full flight as caught by a wing camera. At left: An AD-1 Skyraider fires six rockets and the camera recorded their flight characteristics for the research engineers. Efficiency of new weapons is increased and perfected through such use of photography. Photographs from *U. S. Navy, U. S. Air Force* and the *Naval Ordnance Test Station*, Inyokern.

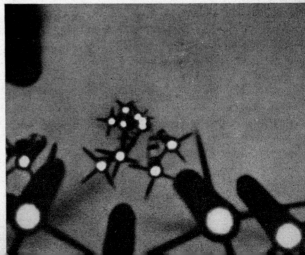

With photographic methods, the human element is eliminated. With photography we can delve into the unseen and magnify or compress time or can slow down or speed up movement. Moreover, it has the ability to compress large areas into small spaces.

It does more than appraise the surfaces of objects. Using radiography it pierces their interiors, producing a weapon of inestimable value in diagnosing sickness. The interior inspection of metal parts and components is possible, eliminating costly failures from internally faulty parts. Photography not only looks at and into objects, it can analyze them at a flip of a switch and at the speed of light—assuring strict adherence to specification without costly stand-by time.

That photography has become so important is a credit to the photographic industry and its tens of thousands of highly skilled workers, and to the men and women who are expert in putting this specialized equipment to work.

Before industry can produce it must develop or find a source of power and raw materials. With photography at work in fields of exploration on the surface of the earth, beneath the water and high in the air—we can locate these essentials as well as map underground oil and mineral resources. With aerial mapping, the best choice of location of a giant hydro-electric dam can be made—faster and cheaper. Aerial surveys pinpoint the routes of powerlines from turbine to industry. They reveal to engineers' trained eyes, new routes for highways and railways, locations for new airfields. Even the site of a factory is sometimes plotted with the all-encompassing facilities of the aerial camera, whose single and multiple eyes reveal the contours and elevations of the terrain in two or three-dimensions as desired. The cameras in the sky record the extent and limitations of our natural resources—water supply and power and timber, the land itself.

To the farmer raising food for fighting and working men and women, air survey photos help him plan the efficient plowing and planting of his (*Continued on Page 360*)

MYSTERIES OF the supersonic are made visible through photography. At supersonic speeds, the configuration of an aircraft and especially the design of the airfoil present problems unique from those of conventional speed planes. What happens to supersonic air flow over an airfoil must be known and Schlieren photographs like that above provide the desired information, accurately and speedily.

AERIAL PHOTOGRAPHY is of prime importance in many tangents of mobilization—from planning to its application on the battlefront. Modern developments in aerial photography have made it possible to record the camera's views in three dimensions, full color and at tremendous speeds and high altitudes. With photoflash bombs, not even darkness of night limits aerial photography. *U. S. Air Force Photo.*

THESE UNUSUAL photographs below are used to study the amount of energy necessary to ignite a flowing gas and to follow the combustion in minute detail to determine conditions for continued propagation. Recorded for the Navy by Dr. Lowell Olsen, Robert B. Edmondson and Everett L. Gayhart of the Applied Physics Laboratory staff at Johns Hopkins University, these pictures will help clear up mysteries that still surround the roaring combustion chambers of rocket motors and jet engines. The pictures were made by the Schlieren method and show development of a flame from the age of 5.8 to 1112-millionths of a second (microseconds). Two common pins were etched to small size and used as electrodes between which a small spark was produced. In the first picture the gas has been ignited

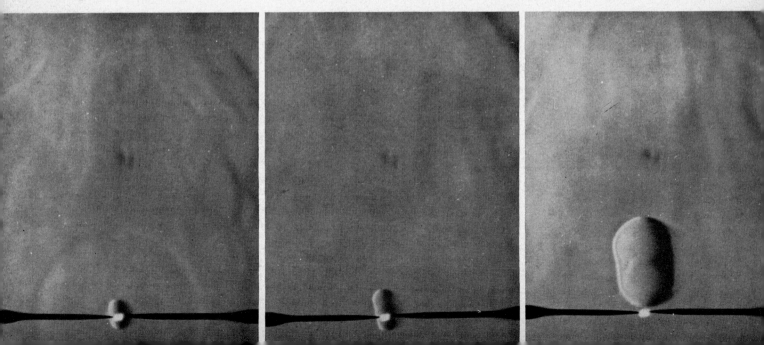

by the spark. The circle around the globule of burning hydrogen is a shock wave produced by the spark. Progressing to the right, the pictures show the flame kernel rapidly expanding until in the last photograph the kernel spreads into the turbulent sides of the stream (of gas) and is broken up. Each combustion stage was photographed separately by use of a delay timer which set off a Schlieren light source at the indicated microseconds after the spark had been created. Because of the short period between the initial spark and when the Schlieren picture is taken, the shutter of the camera must be left open. Therefore, the original spark appears in all the photographs although its duration is less than one millionth of a second. Camera fans will recognize the result as double exposure.

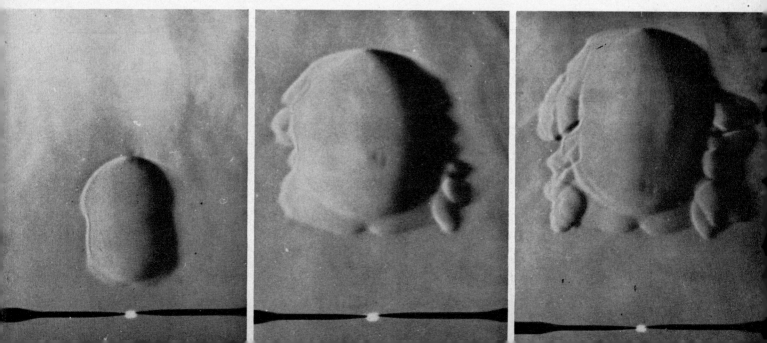

PHOTOGRAPHIC equipment used in mobilization is varied. In above picture is seen an installation for the trimetregon aerial photography process which records the earth's surface from horizon to horizon. *U. S. Air Force Photo.*

HERE IS THE giant Photo-template camera at Glenn Martin Aircraft Company in Maryland. It photographically reproduces accurate working plans on metal. Use of this process has cut costs while increasing production tremendously.

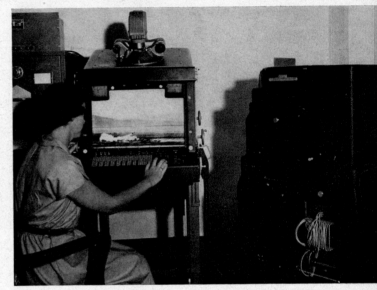

SPECIALIZED problems require unusual photographic equipment. To film underwater movies (often required by the Navy), the unique housing seen in the above illustration was made to protect the camera. *Official U. S. Navy Photo.*

MANY UNUSUAL devices for assessment of film images have been developed at Inyokern Naval Station. Girl is operating an Iconolog viewer which reads cinethcodolite records, tabulates readings, automatically punches data cards.

WING GUN CAMERA, a special 16-millimeter movie camera that operates when machine guns and rockets are fired from planes, is shown being installed by mechanic. It confirms effectiveness of aerial strikes and combat.   *USAF Photo.*

THIS STRANGE device is a long range tracking telescope with a focal length of twenty feet. Its 35 mm. movie camera obtains detailed closeup pictures of missiles many miles distant—for research study.   *U. S. Navy Photograph.*

ROCKETS FIRED at White Sands carry cameras like these to photograph the earth from 130 miles up. The cameras are ejected, at preset altitude in descent of rocket, to parachute safely to earth, films intact. *U. S. Army Photo.*

RIG OF Bell and Howell, Wollensak Fastax and Eastman movie cameras is used to precisely time intervals of exposures of other cameras for minute computations. It was originally designed for A-Bomb tests. *U. S. Air Force Photo.*

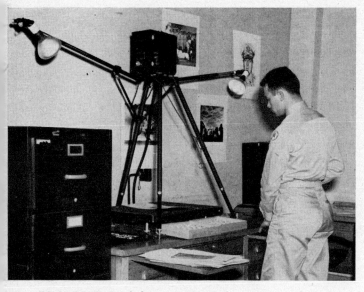

RECORDING of documents and drawings is efficiently accomplished by photographic processes, specifically on microfilm. Microfilming saves up to 99 percent of the space normally used for files, reduces loss. *U. S. Army Photo.*

FIVE SPECIAL four-by-five remote control still cameras are being aligned for photographing tests at the Naval Ordnance Test Station, Inyokern. The battery arrangement was used to solve a particular speed problem. *U. S. Navy Photo.*

INSTRUMENTS can detect and measure phenomena but their findings are only momentary. To make permanent such information for longer and more detailed study, special photographic equipment records and preserves the desired data.

FOR DETERMINATION of structural characteristics of opaque materials such as metals and plastics, an instrument like the Bausch and Lomb Metallograph must be used. Its findings are recorded photographically. *Bausch and Lomb Photo.*

WITH RADIOGRAPHY, internal study of huge castings and parts can be made without destroying the unit. Through use of industrial X-ray or radioactive material with sensitive film positioned as desired (as is being done above), structural defects are revealed. *Ford News Bureau Photo.*

IN ATOMIC research, photography is a major instrument of investigation. Photography wrote the record of the Atom Bomb tests for computation—just as it captured the cosmic rays tracks in a nuclear emulsion shown in the multiple photomicrograph below. *Atomic Energy Commission Photo.*

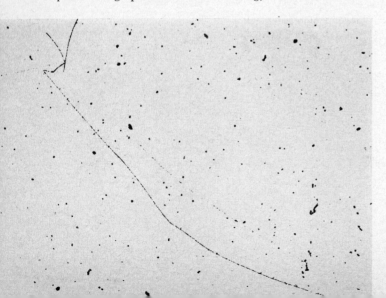

farm and show him where to locate irrigation canals and how to control water and wind erosion of his precious soil.

At planning levels, photographic materials and machines rapidly and accurately duplicate engineering drawings, specifications, records and other essential data. Not always is there a camera involved for the word photography means *to write with light.* It is at this stage that the reproduction processes like blueprinting and the Kodagraph, Ozalid and Xerography methods are the efficient tools doing the task. Simultaneously and continuing through every step of the way in every segment of the mobilization effort, photostat and microfilm machines perform endless wonders of recording. Microfilming is a method of photographing any paper record onto film, thus reducing storage space. Ten thousand engineering drawings can be held in one hand—when recorded on film. Microfilmed records require about 1% of the space required by the original files and provide easier and quicker reference.

Before the prototype of any mobilization product can be made and used for production tooling, a great amount of research must be compiled so that production models will do the job for which they were designed. At research levels, photography is a major instrument. It is at this investigatory stage where the invisible must be made visible, where time must be slowed down (Continued on Page 386)

KODACHROME TRANSPARENCY

KODACHROME TRANSPARENCY

A Frame for Memory

Photographers are fortunate, for when they encounter
something memorable—a day, a place, a scene, a companion
—they have, easily, the means with which to make
that memory live. Kodak color films make these memories
far more vivid, more re-enjoyable.

EASTMAN KODAK COMPANY

Rochester 4, N. Y.

For roll-film cameras	**KODACOLOR FILM** **KODAK EKTACHROME FILM**	
For miniature cameras	**KODACOLOR FILM** **KODACHROME FILM**	
For sheet-film cameras	**KODAK EKTACHROME FILM**	

Kodak
TRADE-MARK

Shortest Route

...from Scene to Color Print

Kodacolor Film gives you the short, one-two-three route to excellent color prints and enlargements—original scene, complementary color negative, and final full-color print. It's a direct process—a thrifty process— and the quality of today's Kodacolor Prints will bring you a pleasant surprise. Kodacolor is convenient, too—it has superior speed, superior exposure latitude for a color film, and comes in both types—Daylight, and Type A for flood and flash. All popular roll-film sizes, plus No. 828 miniature. Add Kodacolor Film now to your color team—you have a treat in store for you.

**FROM YOUR
KODACOLOR NEGATIVE***

- Standard 3½-inch Kodacolor Prints
- Kodacolor Enlargements to 11x14
- Black-and-white prints
  (on Kodak Velox Paper)
- Black-and-white enlargements
  (on Kodabromide Paper)

* Kodacolor Film is developed at no added charge. Kodacolor Prints and Enlargements in full color are ordered separately, in any quantity, through your Kodak dealer. Kodak does not supply black-and-white prints from Kodacolor negatives.

◀ *From a Kodacolor Enlargement*

Kodak
TRADE-MARK

MONOCHROME TO *Flexichrome*

Sheer magic—that's the Kodak Flexichrome Process for full-color prints and enlargements. You start with any good black-and-white negative . . . make a straight black-and-white print on Kodak Flexichrome Film . . . transfer the film emulsion to any paper you like . . . then apply colors which *physically replace* the black-and-white image with a full-color image, while retaining all photographic quality and crispness of detail! You get rich, beautiful color prints—at moderate cost—and you have complete flexibility in selecting and modifying the color scheme. Read the full story of this rewarding process in the new Kodak Flexichrome Data Book, available at your Kodak dealer's. ▶

EASTMAN KODAK COMPANY
ROCHESTER 4, N. Y.

Picture of a happy man . . .

When you peel back the last matrix and your Dye Transfer Print stands fully revealed . . .

When the colorful scene you enjoyed and recorded on a bit of Kodachrome Film comes so magnificently to life on the projection screen at home or at the club . . .

Or when the same scene becomes a brilliant cameo on your table viewer . . .

When a favorite monochrome takes on full color as you manipulate the responsive, re-warding Kodak Flexichrome Process . . .

When you discover that Kodacolor Film, the color film you had thought was "only for snapshooters," gives you a beautiful and subtle print . . .

Or when you come to planning a photograph in full color, confident that the means and skill are yours—then you know some of the satisfactions, the real, deep satisfactions which color photography can give.

EASTMAN KODAK COMPANY

Rochester 4, N. Y.

Kodak
TRADE-MARK

The easy way to Better Pictures

"Clowns" by Joseph Janney Steinmetz

"The meter with a MEMORY"

The Superb PR-1
EXPOSURE METER

The greatest show on earth—comes through in rich, real-life colors, as in this shot by Joseph Steinmetz, when you use a General Electric PR-1 meter.

For the PR-1 is your assurance of perfect exposure, better pictures in *every* case . . . movies, stills, color, black and white.

And *so easy to use!* Just press, set, and read. Your PR-1, *the meter with a MEMORY*, does the rest! Complete for reflected or incident light readings. Try it at your dealer's. **$32.50***

Says Joseph Janney Steinmetz, ASMP and Master Photographer—*"For tops in color, exact exposure is a 'must' and magazine photographers have to be right the first time! The General Electric PR-1 Meter assures these results."*

Also dependable, accurate **DW-68** meter . . . at **$24.50***

*Fair traded. Fed. tax incl. General Electric Co., Schenectady 5, N. Y.

*You can put your confidence in*__

GENERAL ⓖⓔ ELECTRIC

606-100

"The Facts of Life"

Getting the facts of life is largely a matter of knowing where to get the facts. Your best source of information are people with the most know-how. The people with the most know-how in printing problems are likely to be those with the broadest background of experience and the most comprehensive equipment and personnel for research and development. To keep in touch with important printing ink information, keep in touch with IPI. You will find the nearest IPI branch conveniently located.

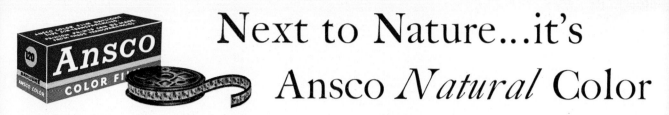

Next to Nature...it's
Ansco *Natural* Color

When you photograph in Ansco Color you get the *whole* picture —the thrilling, living beauty of every scene or subject in gorgeous, natural color—as your eyes see it—rich greens, bright, saturated reds, cool blues. Ansco Color is high-fidelity color. Ansco Color

Film is available in 120 and 620 rolls, 35mm magazines and bulk lengths, sheets, 8 and 16mm magazines, 50 and 100 foot rolls for 16mm movie cameras. Ansco, Binghamton, N. Y. A Division of General Aniline & Film Corporation. *"From Research to Reality."*

for the advancement of 35mm photography as a fine art...

the brilliant *new*

argus C-4

An Argus C-4 picture

Here is Argus' finest achievement—a brilliant, new contribution to the field of modern 35mm photography. Here is a camera tested and acclaimed by experts nationwide...a camera designed and engineered for those who appreciate the fine points of picture-taking.

For fine 35mm color photography— The new Argus C-4 offers you a superb new Cintar f:2.8 lens that, even in failing light, delivers brilliantly crisp results...is outstanding for its quality of resolution and extraordinary depth of field.

Argus C-4 also gives you a special shutter with larger working parts that mean less wear, longer life, consistent accuracy—so essential to good color photography.

For black-and-white candid photography— With the new Argus C-4's combined view-rangefinder, you sight and focus simultaneously through a single, brilliant eyepiece...capture those fleeting candid shots that other cameras so often miss. And the fast C-4 f:2.8 lens, without flash, achieves the most unusual black-and-white pictures under "impossible" lighting conditions.

100% synchronized for flash photography

At *all* shutter speeds, Argus C-4's built-in flash synchronization accommodates *all* flash lamps. The handy clip-on flash unit with push-button lamp ejector mounts conveniently on top of the camera for perfect light coverage; a positive locking device holds it firmly in place to insure the best possible flash results.

The brilliant, new Argus C-4 is now available in limited quantity. We urge you to see it...to prove to yourself that, whatever phase of fine 35mm photography you pursue, Argus C-4 is truly a remarkable camera.

Argus Cameras, Inc., Ann Arbor, Michigan

argus

Argus C-4—$99.50 (incl. Fed. Tax) Case, $7.50; Flash Unit, $10.00. Prices subject to change without notice.

Great Picture

BY ANSEL ADAMS

This appealing photographic study is one of many pictures Ansel Adams has made with the new HASSELBLAD Camera. Famed for his distinguished practice and teaching of photographic technics, Mr. Adams has found in the HASSELBLAD an instrument to match the requirements of the perfectionist.

Great Camera

BY HASSELBLAD

If you are looking for the ultimate in a camera — the 2¼ x 2¼ HASSELBLAD reflex merits your interest. Here is an instrument, crafted in Sweden, with built-in refinements that will bring to your picture making a new range . . . a new sureness. Interchangeable lenses, interchangeable roll-film magazines, automatic controls, speeds to 1/1600 second, built-in flash — these are but a few of the features that make the HASSELBLAD a "must" for your personal inspection.

PRICES—The camera, with 80 mm Kodak Ektar f/2.8 Lens and roll-film magazine, $548. Accessory 135 mm Kodak Ektar f/3.5 Lens, $282, and 250 mm (10 in.) Zeiss Opton Sonnar Lens f/4, $480. Prices include Federal Tax.

Write for the descriptive HASSELBLAD booklet to

Willoughbys

Dept. B
110 West 32nd Street
New York 1, N. Y.

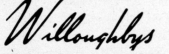

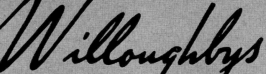

The illustration at the right was made
for Cunningham and Walsh in both Black and White
and Color. The illustration below was made for
Doherty, Clifford Shenfield, Inc., in Black and White.

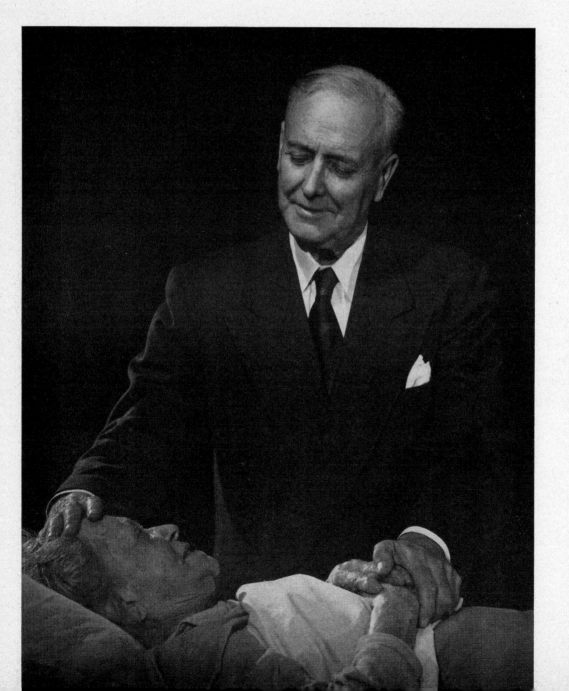

PHOTOGRAPHIC ILLUSTRATION
146 East 56th Street, New York 22, N. Y.
Telephone: PLaza 9-87340

To save you hours in the darkroom...
we spent years in the lab!

Out of the Mallinckrodt research laboratories..come these new ready-and-easy-to-use developers and fixers:

PICTONE® . . . . . . the universal film and paper developer
ULTRATONE® . . . . the fine grain film developer
SOFTONE® . . . . . the low-contrast film developer
CONTRATONE® . . . the high-contrast and process film developer
JIFFIX® . . . . the ultra rapid, acid-hardening fixer

Each is the culmination of over three-quarters of a century's experience and years of dogged, "never-be-satisfied" research. Each will save you time and trouble. Try them and see why other photographers are so enthusiastic!

May we send you detailed data sheets?

Mallinckrodt®

MALLINCKRODT CHEMICAL WORKS

Mallinckrodt St., St. Louis 7, Mo. • 72 Gold St., New York 8, N. Y.

CHICAGO • CINCINNATI • CLEVELAND • LOS ANGELES • MONTREAL • PHILADELPHIA • SAN FRANCISCO

Manufacturers of Medicinal, Photographic, Analytical and Industrial Fine Chemicals

HOW TO GIVE YOUR PICTURES A *Professional Look* OF QUALITY

To assure finest work at all times, many photographers use these dependable Du Pont Photographic Products exclusively:

"VELOUR BLACK" PHOTOGRAPHIC PROJECTION PAPER—favorite professional enlarging paper with sensitive emulsion that reacts to slightest differences in negative density. Grade 1 Soft . . . for contrasty negatives. Grade 2 Normal . . . for average negatives. Grade 3 Medium Hard . . . for flat negatives. Grade 4 Contrast . . . for extremely flat negatives.

"VARIGAM" VARIABLE CONTRAST PHOTOGRAPHIC PAPER—a unique paper providing ten degrees of contrast by selection of the proper filters. Basic 5A Set of Filters; Supplementary 5B Set; Complete Set 10C.

WARMTONE TYPE 9034—an entirely new projection paper. Gives you rich, and radiant pictures with soft, warm tones. Its toning properties are superb. Already a favorite among leading professional photographers.

"APEX" PHOTOGRAPHIC CONTACT PAPER—a popular commercial and photo-finishing paper available in nine surfaces and six degrees of contrast. Professional "Apex" in surfaces BB, DL, EL and Y is ideal for warm-tone portrait work.

HIGH SPEED PAN—TYPE 428—produces top-quality negatives under the most adverse lighting. Permits extremely fast shutter speed or stopping way down for depth and sharpness. ASA daylight 160; tungsten 125.

"ARROW" PAN—high speed; high red sensitive. Ideal for mass portraiture with daylight or fluorescent lighting and flash exposures. ASA daylight 160; tungsten 125.

"X-F" PAN—medium speed; medium fine grain; normal scale. Balanced color sensitivity. Best suited to studio portraiture and illustrative photography with tungsten light. Recommended for color separation negatives. ASA daylight 50; tungsten 32.

FINE GRAIN PAN—maximum speed consistent with fine grain. Balanced color sensitivity. Ideal for murals and specialized uses in industrial and scientific photography; photomicrography; commercial copying. ASA daylight 32; tungsten 20.

PROCESS PAN—extremely high contrast for line work; copying. ASA daylight 16; tungsten 10.

TESTED CHEMICAL PREPARATIONS: 53-D — All Purpose Developer • 55-D—Standard Paper Developer • 16-D—Film Developer • 16-DR—Replenisher for 16-D Developer • 1-F — Acetic Acid Fixer • Wash Test Solution for checking hypo elimination after washing.

today's film commercials

The latest commercial in the series (created by Sarra, Inc.) for the Pet Milk Company catches the excitement of screaming newspaper headlines, and tempers it with the human touch. The new label with a series of enticing milk recipes is the "star". Later sequences feature shots of mouth-watering dishes, all prepared and ready to serve a hungry family. There's news value in this series, as well as prompt, complete brand identification.

ADVERTISER
Pet Milk Company

AGENCY
Gardner Advertising Company

PRODUCED BY

SARRA, INC.
NEW YORK: 200 EAST 56th STREET
CHICAGO: 16 EAST ONTARIO STREET

These 20 delightful seconds are alive with whimsical animation. The famous P.O.C. Advertising character performs on his familiar bicycle and makes a telling motion picture poster for a new brew by the Pilsener Brewing Company of Cleveland. Clever detail enlivens the chorus praising "That new '51 flavor". Animation doubles the effectiveness of the catchy selling jingles.

ADVERTISER
Pilsener Brewing Company
Cleveland, Ohio

AGENCY
Meldrum & Fewsmith, Inc.
Cleveland, Ohio

PRODUCED BY

SARRA, INC.
NEW YORK: 200 EAST 56th STREET
CHICAGO: 16 EAST ONTARIO STREET

Sun Oil Company's hard selling theme "It's Road Tested" is given gay visualization in animated cartoon—a dancing can tripping along a country road with signposts pointing in opposite directions, Quebec and Key West. There's plenty of interesting action to dramatize the Sunoco selling points and the entire commercial drives home its message with force and distinction.

ADVERTISER
Sun Oil Company

AGENCY
Hewitt, Ogilvy, Benson & Mather, Inc.

PRODUCED BY

SARRA, INC.
NEW YORK: 200 EAST 56th STREET
CHICAGO: 16 EAST ONTARIO STREET

Here's the latest Palmolive spot. A delightful concoction of hard fact and pleasant romance that spells sales for Palmolive. Through a magic mirror, a song and dance skit dramatizes the "Let Your Beauty Be Seen" jingle. Throughout, a giant cake of Palmolive shares the spotlight with live talent—an effective device to play up brand identification.

ADVERTISER
Colgate-Palmolive-Peet Company

AGENCY
Ted Bates & Company

PRODUCED BY

SARRA, INC.
NEW YORK: 200 EAST 56th STREET
CHICAGO: 16 EAST ONTARIO STREET

The universal summertime appeal of dining outdoors is made doubly enticing in this series of commercials. In fast moving sequences luscious barbecued favorites are given the extra zest of a generous spicing with French's Mustard. Good, snappy voice-over selling commercials coordinate well with the film and enhance the sales punch of the clever zoom-in signature that gets across brand identification with emphasis.

ADVERTISER
R. T. French Co.

AGENCY
J. Walter Thompson Co.

PRODUCED BY

SARRA, INC.
NEW YORK: 200 EAST 56th STREET
CHICAGO: 16 EAST ONTARIO STREET

SPECIALISTS IN VISUAL ADVERTISING

Keep your eye on the series produced for Gold Seal Glass Wax through Campbell-Mithun, Inc. Here's prize-winning technique in imaginative photography to dramatize in live action the product's multiple uses, easy cleaning action and outstanding results. There's a neat integration too, of other products made by Gold Seal—Wood Cream, Self Polishing Floor Wax and the newly-launched Snowy Bleach. Another prize-winning commercial in the 9th Annual Awards Competition of the Chicago Federated Advertising Club.

ADVERTISER
Gold Seal Company

AGENCY
Campbell-Mithun, Inc.

PRODUCED BY
SARRA, INC.
NEW YORK: 200 EAST 56th STREET
CHICAGO: 16 EAST ONTARIO STREET

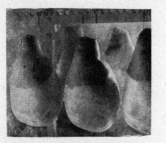

Prize-winning technique puts sales punch 'a plenty in a one-minute spot for Swift Premium Ham. The 9th Annual Awards Competition of the Chicago Federated Advertising Club voted it an award. Photographic effects intensify a feeling of suspense in the live action. The product's multiple uses in easy sequence are contrasted tellingly with appetizing shots of luscious fully baked hams. Brand name identification is extremely well handled throughout.

ADVERTISER
Swift & Company

AGENCY
J. Walter Thompson Co.
Chicago, Ill.

PRODUCED BY
SARRA, INC.
NEW YORK: 200 EAST 56th STREET
CHICAGO: 16 EAST ONTARIO STREET

"What a dish" is the theme for the Grennan Bakeries' film series, and makes clever use of a variety of boy-girl situations to stress luscious looking baked goods for dessert.
Close ups of appealing youngsters enjoying cake and pies do a real job of suggestive selling. A 60-second and a 20-second version of this commercial both sparkle with life. In fact, one of this series won a coveted Award in the 9th Annual Awards Competition of the Chicago Federated Advertising Club.

ADVERTISER
Purity Bakeries Corp.

AGENCY
Young & Rubicam, Inc.

PRODUCED BY
SARRA, INC.
NEW YORK: 200 EAST 56th STREET
CHICAGO: 16 EAST ONTARIO STREET

These fast paced live-action commercials produced for Armour & Company play up appetite appeal with fine looking main dish platters. The selling story for Cloverbloom Turkeys moves smoothly through stop motion and live action with plenty of mouth-watering close-ups. Name identification gets an ingenious touch that boosts brand recognition. This commercial—one of a series for Armour & Company—won an award in the 9th Annual Awards Competition of the Chicago Federated Advertising Club.

ADVERTISER
Armour & Company

AGENCY
Foote, Cone & Belding

PRODUCED BY
SARRA, INC.
NEW YORK: 200 EAST 56th STREET
CHICAGO: 16 EAST ONTARIO STREET

The opening of the Lucky Strike Hit Parade combines stop motion and animation in 45 seconds of charm and impact. It is one of the best examples of radio copy being brought to life through imaginative visualization. The catchy Lucky Strike jingle gets effective handling . . . with the staff of music dissolving to a spinning disc, a juke box and sheet music . . . to illustrate visually the basis for the Lucky Strike tabulations. This film commercial was honored by exhibition at the 30th Annual Exhibit of the Art Directors Club of New York. It was created by Sarra, Inc. from story board to finished production.

ADVERTISER
Lucky Strike Cigarettes

AGENCY
Batten, Barton, Durstine & Osborn, Inc.

PRODUCED BY
SARRA, INC.
NEW YORK: 200 EAST 56th STREET
CHICAGO: 16 EAST ONTARIO STREET

SPECIALISTS IN VISUAL ADVERTISING

*From a series of pictures of the Southwest
made exclusively for Haloid
by Gibbons of Banff.*

YOUR NEGATIVES COME TO LIFE
on Haloid Photographic Papers

All the drama and detail you have captured in your negatives
are brought to life with realistic beauty on Haloid Photographic
Papers. In processing, Haloid Papers are known for their ex-
ceptional latitude, development tolerance and print control.

Write for complete information on Haloid Photographic Papers.

THE HALOID COMPANY
51-202 HALOID STREET, ROCHESTER 3, N. Y.
BRANCH OFFICES: Atlanta, Boston, Chicago, Dallas, Denver, Detroit, Los Angeles,
New York, Philadelphia, Pittsburgh, St. Louis, San Francisco, Seattle, Washington, D. C.

Photographic Papers • Photo-Copying Machines • Photocopy Papers
Negative Materials for the Graphic Arts • **XeroX Products for xerography**

The pages of history
are pictured by
GRAFLEX

Graflex—leaders for 60 years in the development and manufacture of fine cameras and equipment for the press, professional, commercial, military, and advanced amateur photographer.

Sam Caldwell
St. Louis Post-Dispatch

International News Photos

Herb Scharfman, INP.

GRAFLEX *Prize-Winning Cameras*
Rochester 8, N. Y.

Graflex Cameras ★ Pacemaker Speed Graphic ★ Pacemaker Crown Graphic ★ Century Graphic ★ Graphic View ★ Graflite Flash

Sam Shere, INP.

379

Wherever You Turn... it's pictures by

Rollei

In the photo publications, the annuals, the news magazines . . . or wherever else the outstanding work of the leaders is shown . . . credit-line after credit-line reads *picture by Rollei*. Because, *more than any other camera*, Rollei furnishes the convenience, fast operation, versatility and precise picture results that leading photographers demand. See automatic Rolleiflex, and the companion Rolleicord, at your dealer's today.

New Auto-Rollei features full synchronization and provision for use of new type Rolleikin 35 mm. adapter.

Burleigh Brooks Company
10 West 46th Street, New York 19, N. Y.

Western States, Alaska and Hawaii:
PONDER & BEST, INC.
1230 So. Grand Ave., Los Angeles 15, Cal.

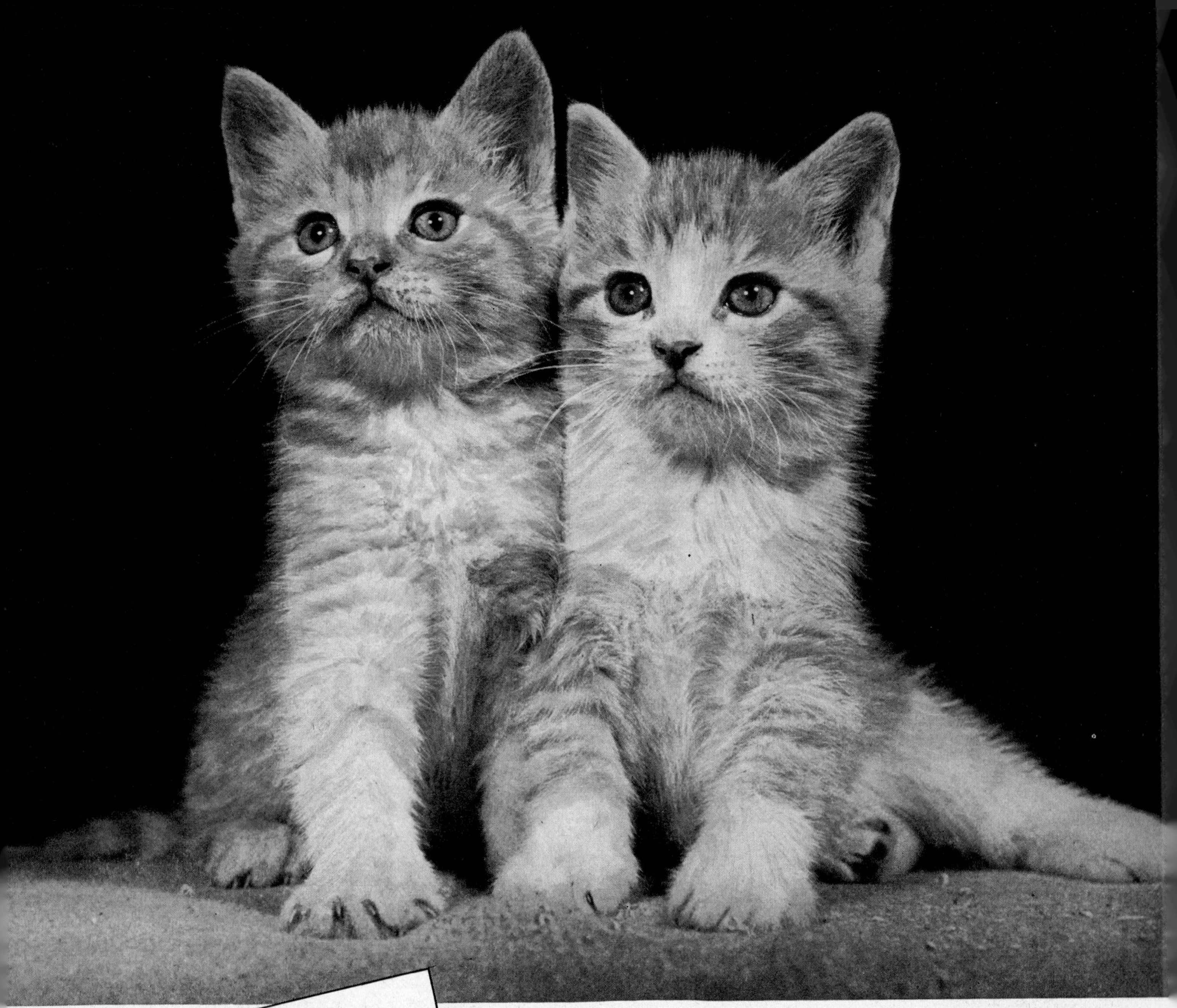

Photo by Walter Chandoha

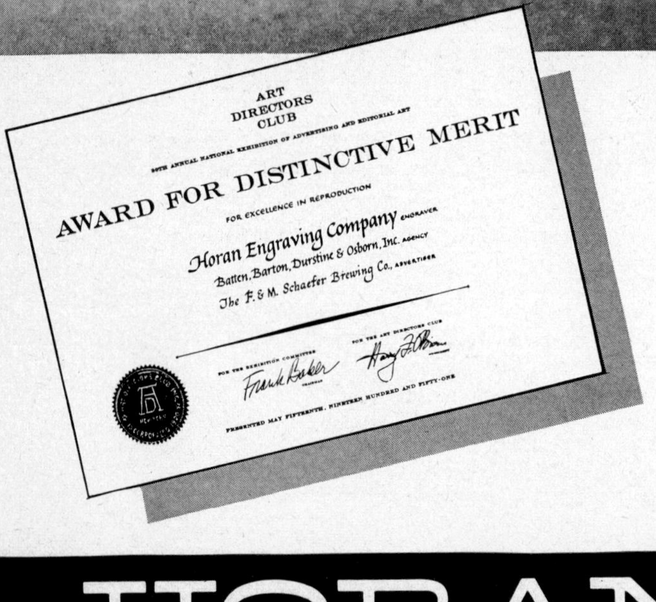
ART
DIRECTORS
CLUB
30TH ANNUAL NATIONAL EXHIBITION OF ADVERTISING AND EDITORIAL ART
AWARD FOR DISTINCTIVE MERIT
FOR EXCELLENCE IN REPRODUCTION
Horan Engraving Company ENGRAVER
Batten, Barton, Durstine & Osborn, Inc. AGENCY
The F. & M. Schaefer Brewing Co., ADVERTISER
PRESENTED MAY FIFTEENTH, NINETEEN HUNDRED AND FIFTY-ONE

SPARKLE . . . CLARITY . . . DETAIL — some of the considerations that won for us this award and influenced U. S. Camera to entrust to us the reproduction of most of the illustrations in this Annual.

HORAN Engraving Company, Inc.

44 WEST 28 STREET, NEW YORK 1, N. Y. • MURRAY HIILL 9-8585

BRANCH OFFICES | 30 FULTON STREET, NEWARK, N. J. • MARKET 2-4172
9 PARKWAY COURT, ALLENTOWN, PA. • ALLENTOWN 4-6718

JANUARY — Winter Sports

FEBRUARY — Parties

MARCH — Hobbies

APRIL — Easter

DECEMBER — Christmas

MAY — Spring Flowers

NOVEMBER — Thanksgiving

JUNE — Graduations · Weddings

OCTOBER — Halloween

SEPTEMBER — Back to School

AUGUST — Vacations

JULY — Gardening

SUPERFLASH BULBS

GIVE YOU YEAR-ROUND FUN WITH YOUR CAMERA

Any time of the day or night, 365 days a year, is picture-taking time—with Superflash. Anywhere, in any weather, you can keep your camera busy —because the famous bulb with the identifying Blue Dot provides "better than sunlight" for top-grade shooting.

That's one reason more photographers—both professional and amateur—use Superflash than any other flashbulb!

So don't put your camera away because the day is cloudy or because the sun has set . . . and don't miss the fun of shooting scenes indoors. Enjoy your camera more all year round. Get better pictures—with Superflash!

ONLY SUPERFLASH BRINGS YOU ALL 4 . . .

1. **BLUE DOTS FOR SURE SHOTS!** Blue Dot is your protection against damaged bulbs.
2. **QUICK-FLASH FILAMENT** means sure flash even when batteries are weak.
3. **EVEN-LIGHT BULB SHAPE** distributes brighter light more evenly.
4. **SAFETY JACKET** inside and outside of bulb guards against shattering.

Blue Dots for Sure Shots!

SYLVANIA

1740 Broadway, New York 19, New York

There's a Superflash bulb for every type of camera and for both black and white and color film.

PHOTOLAMPS; LIGHT BULBS; RADIO TUBES; TELEVISION PICTURE TUBES; ELECTRONIC PRODUCTS; ELECTRONIC TEST EQUIPMENT; FLUORESCENT TUBES, FIXTURES, SIGN TUBING, WIRING DEVICES; TELEVISION SETS

383

"The Bottle Tree" By AXEL POIGNANT

ISAAC GOLDMANN COMPANY

A COMPLETE PRINTING SERVICE

Letterpress  *Offset*

630 ELEVENTH AVENUE   NEW YORK 36, NEW YORK

PRINTERS OF U. S. CAMERA ANNUAL • 1952

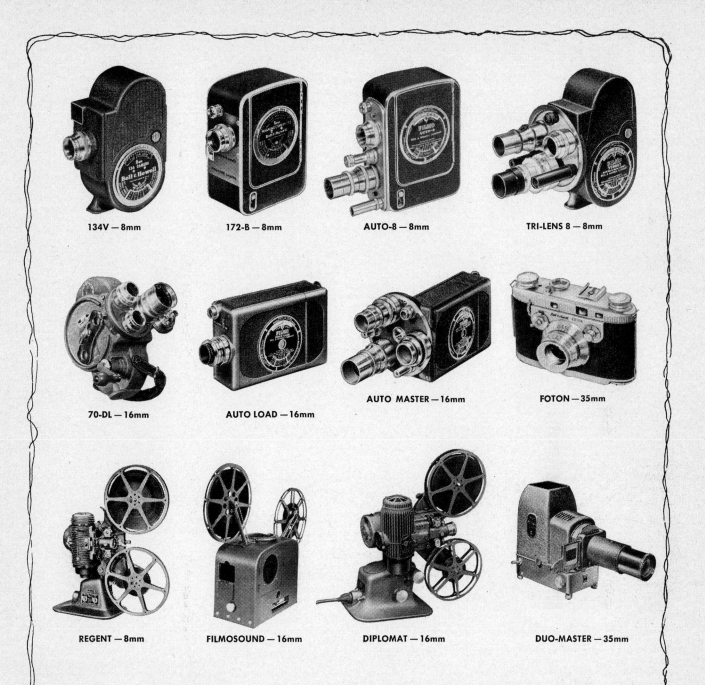

134V — 8mm 172-B — 8mm AUTO-8 — 8mm TRI-LENS 8 — 8mm

70-DL — 16mm AUTO LOAD — 16mm AUTO MASTER — 16mm FOTON — 35mm

REGENT — 8mm FILMOSOUND — 16mm DIPLOMAT — 16mm DUO-MASTER — 35mm

A page from a fine family album

Newest member of the family—

THE "200"—16mm magazine loading camera.
Winner of the coveted Society of Motion Picture Art Directors Award. Interchangeable lens; positive viewfinder; continuous-run lock; single frame release; ratchet winding.

Also Swifturn 2-lens turret model with matching positive viewfinder.

Bell & Howell movie equipment is designed to do one thing: give the best results. Cameras and projectors alike are precision-made, easy to operate, and are dependable performers in every way. This complete line takes care of every movie-making requirement—8 or 16mm—silent or sound. And every Bell & Howell product is guaranteed for life.

GUARANTEED FOR LIFE
During life of product, any defects in workmanship or material will be remedied free (except transportation).

You buy for life when you buy

Bell & Howell

7121A McCormick Road, Chicago 45, Illinois

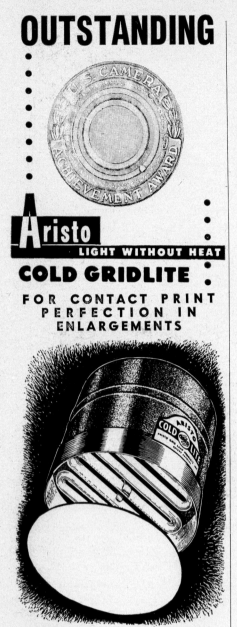
HALSMAN

(Continued from Page 18)

Here's a photographer's photographer; a versatile fellow as canny with his camera as he is capable with an unbridled wit, a commodity he copes with on frequent occasions.

As you can see on pages 18 through 31, "The Perfect Fool", "Charley's Aunt", "Robert the Roue from Reading, Pa.", "Jimmy, The Well-Dressed Man", Einstein, Picasso, Cocteau and Weegee all gather a glow that is each character's own illumination as soon as they appear in photo print by Halsman. And don't let these bantering words beguile you into thinking that Philippe Halsman is mainly jest and gesture. If Durante is an artist; if Dali is an escapist; if Swanson is an actress; if Einstein is a physicist, then Halsman is a fine—and rare—photographer. This is especially true of his portrait work, where in spite of his facility with the camera he shows great depth of perception. In his portraits, he attempts to capture, not recreate or stage, the essence of the human being—the personality and character behind the features.

He is also the inventor of an excellent camera called the Fairchild-Halsman, an equally excellent book called *The Frenchman* (many months on the best-seller lists) and thanks to *The Frenchman,* the innovator and instigator of a succession of picture books ($1.00 per, paper cover).

The man is insidious. If he photographs babies, baby photographers are distressed. If he photographs animals other animals are envious. And when he photographs females —which he often does—every male in America is jealous—a reasonable condition impossible to adjust. These are a few of the reasons why Philippe Halsman's pictures introduce U.S. Camera's pages this year. The editor thinks they look very good here—even better than they have on other pages of U.S. Camera Annual every year since he arrived in these parts to become a leading photo citizen of the "good old You Es Aye".

Variety is also the spice of Halsman's camera use. For several years he and Salvador Dali, an old friend, have been collaborating. The latest of their joint efforts, together with the production shots are presented on pages 20-22. About these, Halsman says: "Dali made the drawing of a skull which was composed of nudes *(See pages 20-21)* and then we tried to reproduce it on film with live models. In my studio we built a special platform which could be adjusted to different heights. Then came the problem of selecting the models. Some girls with very good figures had to be rejected because their hips were not wide enough. After finally selecting the nine we wanted, we tackled the main job of arranging the models to form the shape of the skull. This took more than three hours to accomplish, and was complicated by the fact that the poses were strenuous and the girls could only hold them for a short time. During all these preparations, one Rollei was connected with speed lights turned toward the ceiling and from time to time my wife, Yvonne, and Gene Cook would take shots.

"When the right poses had been finally arrived at and everything corrected, the actual picture *(page 22)* was taken with a 4X5 camera, stopped down to f/22, with the strobe lights. Twenty seconds of actual photographing had required more than three hours of posing and three days of work."

The photographs of Imogene Coca *(page 19)* and Ed Wynn, Jimmy Durante, Ray Bolger, Jack Carson, Milton Berle, Bobby Clark, Sid Caesar, Eddie Cantor and Fred Allen were all taken for NBC television. The photos of Connie Mack *(page 30),* and show girls of "Peep Show" *(pages 28-9)* were taken for *Life.*

PHOTO

(Continued from Page 360)

or speeded up, where space must be conquered and the activities of even the sun and moon must be probed for their secrets.

Particularly useful to engineer and scientist are the various forms of high speed and time-lapse photography; radiography, photomicrography, metallography and spectrography.

With high speed motion pictures filmed at thousands of frames per *second,* action time is magnified hundreds of times. Conversely, with time-lapse movies, it is possible to telescope the slow action occurring over a long period of time down to any desired fraction of minutes and seconds. There are innumerable cameras of varying design which have been made for particular high speed problems, each serving to permanently record the invisible action of moving parts, objects and explosions.

With time magnification photography, engineers can evaluate the efficiency of an airplane or ship, designed in miniature, and accurately predict the performance of the actual craft. Compressing time through photography permits investigations into the growth of plants and similar actions which must be clearly seen in order to determine the effectiveness of vitamins or other scientific discoveries.

With spectrography, scientists have determined the makeup of our universe and have been able to harness the atom through such findings. Through spectrography, metallography and photomicrography the minute structures of metals, alloys, plastics and other opaque materials have been made to give up their secrets. With such visual information the technicians develop and improve the quality of construction materials and maintain control of desired quality for specific structural requirements. In this field the electron microscope has become a most important tool, all its tremendously magnified observations being captured on film. The power of its vision, in addition to aiding industry, is responsible for important strides in medical and scientific fields. It has already proven its usefulness to the farmer, its penetrating eye revealing formerly unknown microscopic organisms which cause plant diseases. Knowing the cause enables the scientist to discover

(Continued on Page 388)

A BATTERY OF motion picture cameras which were used to record the atomic explosions at Bikini. *U. S. Army-Navy Photo.*

RAY ATKESON MASTERS A MOUNTAIN

WITH HIS POLAROID LAND CAMERA

Ray Atkeson's specialty is "the Northwest in pictures." He's famed for his skill in capturing towering mountains, snow scenes and winter sports on film.

And Ray Atkeson has high praise for his Polaroid picture-in-a-minute Camera. It shows him in just sixty seconds how any photo idea will look. Sharp black and white Polaroid prints are developed right in the camera, dry and ready for an on-the-spot check, all in sixty seconds. If the picture isn't exactly right, he knows the reason why...right away!

This striking view of Mount Millicent in the Wasatch Mountains near Salt Lake City was taken in the early morning from Alpine Rose Lodge. Atkeson used his Polaroid Camera, on a tripod, set at shutter #4. He focused at 50 feet to give maximum depth and used the yellow filter from the Polaroid Filter Kit. The picture was simple to take, magnificent to see!

Amateurs as well as professional photographers are getting better results—and lots more fun—with Polaroid Land Cameras. In brilliance of highlights and depth of blacks...in crispness of detail...the new type 41 Polaroid black-and-white prints challenge comparison with expert darkroom production.

Whether a beginner or professional . . . visit your dealer and ask to see the Polaroid Land Camera in action.

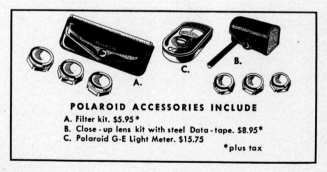

POLAROID ACCESSORIES INCLUDE
A. Filter kit. $5.95 *
B. Close - up lens kit with steel Data-tape. $8.95*
C. Polaroid G-E Light Meter. $15.75
*plus tax

POLAROID® *Land* CAMERA
The world's most exciting camera

Polaroid ® by Polaroid Corporation

387

PHOTO

(Continued from Page 386)

the cure and many times—the method of prevention. The electron microscope has made possible similar achievements in medicine. Radiography is growing in its industrial applications every day. With X-rays and other radio-active materials, research men can detect flaws in objects—without having to tear apart and destroy the object. Photography as applied to stress analysis is an additional means of pre-detecting potential failures and instituting immediate correction. When such detection is possible with tremendous castings and other massive units—the saving in time and cost is a big factor in greater production at later stages.

Hand in hand with research is the necessity and responsibility of testing materials and products. More than anything else, photography is the essential tool by which the scientist, engineer, physicist and metallurgist evaluates and determines whether the efforts of planning and research have been successful. All phases of functional photography are brought to bear in testing—from simple still picture records to high speed films, from instrument recording to reproduction—each contributes to the end result. Photography writes the record of an A-Bomb test. It reveals the behavior and effects of explosions and the flight of bullets, shells, bombs and rockets—for clear cut, accurate study.

Cameras in the cockpits of new planes and machines film the needles of instruments and present a more comprehensive and reliable report than could be made by the best test pilot or operator. Photography reveals the cause of failures and confirms the success in performance. With such records, production of finer quality tools and equipment for a great mobilization effort—is made possible.

When it has been decided that a particular piece of equipment is to be produced, it is necessary to train people to be able to make the components. Training films, slides, books, manuals — reproduction in printed pages — are photographic tools for the job. Training films, particularly, have made it possible to more clearly show what is to be done and it has been found that such films reduce the length of time required to train a person for a skilled operation. Further, visual instruction is long remembered.

After planning, research, testing and training have occurred—only then can production begin. Photography serves the production line as it does at all other levels. In the aviation industry, and now being applied in other industries, the photo template cameras have speeded up production fantastically. Photolayout methods have cut costs by 75% and time by 90%. In this process, accurate working plans are reproduced on sensitized sheets of metals which then become parts of the actual aircraft — after stamping, drilling, shaping, cutting and other operations are performed as per the detailed drawings and instructions.

It is in the production end that the duplication of engineering drawings made at the planning stages are used. It is here that the harvest in time, money and quality—from the uses of photography—is reaped. And, if the industrial capacity were geared for peaceful rather than potential war production—photography would continue from this point of product attainment—to the actual selling of the goods.

After production, further testing goes on. It is with cameras and films, and other photographic processes, that the final answers are obtained.

With security of topmost concern during a mobilization period, employee and personnel identification is a necessity. Photography does the job better than anything else. When there is cause for police or security investigation, photography helps track down those or that which is sought. And, upon capture, photographs are made for permanent identification.

It is, of course, necessary in a defense effort that the health of the fighting and working men and women be protected. Photography and photographic processes in the medical field and the realm of other sciences are continually used to protect and improve health. Progress is made daily, one of the more recent developments being the introduction of a process by which X-rays can be made within less than a minute. With such equipment, men on the battlefield are given a greater chance for survival after being wounded—and, workmen will also benefit from this faster process of diagnosis. Photography coupled with microscopes constantly probes the invisible to discover the microbes and organisms responsible for illnesses. These findings reduce the number of man hours lost on production and fighting lines.

Photography is a major form of communication. With it in the mobilization effort, the world is being shown what is being done, how it is being done and why it is being done—through news pictures in papers, magazines, books, posters, newsreels and television. Photography is fighting the spread of communism by illustrating the truth.

The proving ground of the importance of photography is, of course, on the battlefield. The products of mobilization are used there. Warfare strategy is planned according to what is available—the men in uniform who have been better trained through the uses of films and slides and other material reproduced by photographic processes; men whose morale is kept at high levels through front line screenings of entertaining motion pictures and by their own hobby of photography, which is encouraged by service-sponsored photo competitions; men whose morale is maintained by pictures from home and—the familiar V-mail. Combat is formulated on the tanks, planes, trucks, ships, cannons, shells, bullets, bombs and rockets—and all the other instruments of killing and destruction—that are on hand, and the performance statistics of such weapons. All of which photography helped to produce and evaluate. Battles are fought with maps recorded by

NEWEST of the reproduction processes playing an important part in mobilization effort is Xerography. Simple equipment seen in above photo duplicates plans and documents speedily. *Photo from Haloid Co.*

CAMERAS are used to study stresses of models in wind tunnel. *Photo from Boeing.*

aerial cameras mounted in high speed planes which roar over enemy territory and bring back detailed information of terrain, location and strength of the enemy. Aerial photography confirms the results of bombing and shelling attacks; it penetrates camouflage and has a multitude of other military uses. Movie cameras mounted in fighting planes record bombing and strafing attacks and confirm enemy "kills" in the air. Cameras on aircraft carriers keep a record of approaches and landings—to improve the skill of the pilots.

Everywhere in the battle zone—photography uncomplainingly does its job, efficiently. The combat photographer shows us how the equipment we produce—pay off. His pictures, still and movie, bring home the impact of war in newspapers, magazines and periodicals; in our theaters and on the television screens.

Major portions of the industry are geared, today, to provide photographic equipment and materials essential in the mobolization effort. This will increase as the defense buildup moves ahead, and — wherever a new task for photography is discovered, it will be skillfully and speedily performed. With photography as a tool of an endless number of uses and applications, the success of the mobilization effort is assured.

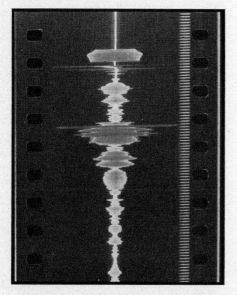

CONTINOUS FILM cameras with visual time track on the film (at right) allow for the permanent recording, and minute and accurate study and interpretation of phenomena. *Official Photograph U.S. Navy.*

KALART Invention Keeps You From Missing Flash Pictures

B-C Flash Unit with built-in test light shows —BEFORE YOU SHOOT —whether flash lamps and batteries are OK

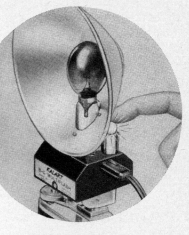

The light that says "OK"
Test light is located directly back of reflector—and is ready to use instantly. Simply press it down after inserting flash lamp. A brief flash is a signal that battery and flash lamps are good.

THE new Kalart B-C Flash Unit eliminates the most common cause of flash failure — *weak batteries.* The flash lamps are fired not by batteries but by tiny and p o w e r f u l battery-capacitor power pack. This new superpower method of firing flash lamps shoots the current to them with a sudden wallop. It assures peak lamp performance—whether you are using one lamp, two lamps . . . or up to six lamps on long extension wires. And you can forget about replacing batteries for two years or longer.

In addition, the Kalart B-C Flash Unit is the *only flash equipment* that enables you to make sure— *before you trip the shutter*—that *every lamp* is good regardless of whether you are using single flash, two lamps or a six-lamp extension hookup.

Further to simplify the use of extension flash, each Kalart B-C Unit is wired in series and provided with patent-pending "Self-Closing" outlets. This assures positive synchronization of 2 to 6 lamps; also permits firing only one lamp in Flash Unit when not using extension flash.

PRICE
$15.95
complete including battery and capacitor
Kalart B-C Flash Unit on Agfa Ventura. For cameras with accessory mounting shoes, Unit is supplied with correct style bracket. For other cameras, a rubber-cushioned attaching bracket that screws into tripod socket is supplied. Unit for cameras with built-in sync, $15.95, complete.

Kalart B-C Flash Unit and one Extension Unit on reflex camera. Correct connecting cords or synchronizers are available for all types of cameras —with or without built-in sync. A Kalart B-C Flash Unit **and** Extension Unit **cost less** than many 3-cell battery flash guns alone.

Send for free booklets. Just name those you want: Kalart B-C Flash Unit—Focuspot for Rollei—Range Finder and Focuspot—Kalart II Camera. Dept. 1-52, Kalart, Plainville, Conn.

KALART

THE HELL BOMB

(*Continued from Page 290*)

fire" might, after all, be lighted on earth. Early studies had revealed that the explosion of an atomic bomb, if it lived up to expectations, would generate a central temperature of about 50,000,000 degrees centigrade. Here, at last, was the promise of realization of the impossible — the 50,000,000 degree match.

The men of Los Alamos thus knew that if the atomic bomb they were just completing for its first test worked as they hoped it would, it could be used as the match to light the deuterium fire. They could build a super-duper bomb of a thousand times the power of the atomic bomb by incorporating deuterium

in the A-bomb, the explosion of which would act as the trigger for the superexplosion. And they also knew that the deuterium bomb held such additional potentialities of terror, beyond its vastly greater blasting and burning power, that the step from the duper to the super would be just as great as the step from TNT to the duper.

The hydrogen bomb, H-bomb, or hell bomb, as the fusion bomb had become popularly known, thus became a reality in the flash of the explosion of the first atomic bomb at 5:30 of the morning of July 16, 1945, on the New Mexico desert. As the men of Los Alamos, of whom I was at that time a privileged member, watched the supramundane light and the apocalyptic mushroom-topped mountain of nuclear fire rising to a height of more than eight miles through

the clouds, they did not have to wait until they checked with their measuring instruments to know that a match sparking a flame of about 50,000,000 degrees centigrade had been lighted on earth for the first time. The size of the fire mountain and the end-of-the-world-like thunder that reverberated all around, told the tale better than any puny man-made instruments.

To light a fire successfully, it is not enough merely to have a match. The match must burn for a time long enough for its flame to act. If you try to light a cigarette in a strong wind, the wind may blow out your match so fast that your cigarette will not light. The same question presents itself here, but on a much greater scale. The match for lighting deuterium—namely, the A-bomb—burns only for about a hundred billionths of a second. Is this time long enough to light the "cigarette" with this one and only "match"?

The question of what type of hydrogen is to be used in the H-bomb therefore hangs on the question of which one of the possible combinations will catch fire by the light of a match that is blown out after an interval of about a hundred billionths of a second.

We can thus see that if deuterium alone is found to be all that is required to set off an H-bomb it will be cheap and relatively easy to make in a short time — both for us and for Russia. Furthermore, such a deuterium bomb would be practically limitless in size. One of a million times the power of the Hiroshima bomb is possible, since deuterium can be extracted in limitless amounts from plain water. On the other hand, if sizable amounts of tritium are found necessary, the cost will be much higher and it will take a considerably longer time, since the production of tritium is very slow and costly.

The radius of destructiveness by the blast of a bomb with a thousand times the energy of the A-bomb will be only ten times greater, since the increase goes by the cube root of the energy. The radius of total destruction by blast in Hiroshima was one mile. Therefore the radius of a superbomb a thousand times more powerful will be ten miles, or a total area of 314 square miles. A bomb a million times the power of the Hiroshima bomb would require 1,000 tons of deuterium. Such a super-superduper could be exploded at a distance from an abandoned, innocent-looking tramp ship. It would have a radius of destruction by blast of 100 miles and a destructive area of more than 30,000 square miles. The time may come when we shall have to search every vessel several hundred miles off shore. And the time may be nearer than we think.

The radius over which the tremendous heat generated by a bomb of a thousandfold the energy would produce fatal burns would be as far as twenty miles from the center of the explosion. This radius increases as the square root, instead of the cube root, of the power. The Hiroshima bomb caused fatal burns at a radius of two thirds of a mile.

The effects of the radiations from a hydrogen bomb are so terrifying that by describing them I run the risk of being branded a fearmonger. Yet facts are facts, and they have been known to scientists for a long time. It would be a disservice to the people if the facts were further denied to them. We have already paid too high a price for a secrecy that now turns out never to have been secret at all.

I can do no better than quote Albert Einstein. "The hydrogen bomb," he said, "appears on the public horizon as a probably attainable goal. . . . If successful, radioactive poisoning of the atmosphere, and hence annihilation of any life on earth, has been

brought within the range of technical possibilities."

The casing of the bomb could be selected with a view to producing, after the neutrons enter it, an especially powerful radioactive substance. Since each artificially made, radioactive element gives out a specific type of radiation and has a definite life span, after which it decays to one half of its radioactivity, the signer of the bomb could rig it in such a way that its explosion would spread into the air a tremendous cloud of specially selected radioactive substances that would give off lethal radiations for a definite period of time. In such a way a large area could be made unfit for human or animal habitation for a definite period of time, months or years.

"It is not even impossible to imagine," in the words of Professor Teller, "that the effects of an atomic war fought with greatly perfected weapons and pushed by utmost determination will endanger the survival of man. . . . . This specific possibility of destruction may help us realize more clearly the probable consequences of an atomic war for our civilization and the possible consequences for the whole human race."

Some scientists and others contend that, because of our great harbor and industrial cities, the hydrogen bomb would be a greater threat to us than to the Soviet, because most Russian cities are much smaller than ours, while her industries are much more dispersed. There may be some truth in this. But on the other hand there are some great advantages on our side. With a strong Navy and good submarine-detecting devices we may have control of the seas and be able to prevent the delivery of the hydrogen bomb by ship or submarine. With a strong Air Force and radar system we could prevent the delivery of hydrogen bombs from the air.

By far the most important advantage the possession of the hydrogen bomb would give us against Russia is its possible use as a tactical weapon against huge land armies. Since they can devastate such large areas, one or two hydrogen bombs, depending on their size, could wipe out entire armies on the march, even before they succeeded in crossing the border of an intended victim. The H-bomb would thus counterbalance if not completely nullify, the one great advantage Russia possesses—huge land armies capable of overrunning western Europe. The bomb might thus serve as the final deterrent to any temptation the Kremlin's rulers may have to invade the Atlantic Pact countries.

Yet no matter how one looks at it, the advent of the H-bomb constitutes the greatest threat to the survival of the human race since the Black Death.

One is reminded of a dinner conversation in Paris in 1869, recorded in the *Journal* of the Goncourt brothers. Some of the famous savants of the day were crystal-gazing into the scientific future a hundred years away. The great chemist Pierre Berthelot predicted that by 1969 "man would know of what the atom is constituted and would be able, at will, to moderate, extinguish, and light up the sun as if it were a gas lamp." (This prophecy has almost come true.) Claude Bernard, the greatest physiologist of the day, saw a future in which "man would be so completely the master of organic law that he would create life [artificially] in competition with God."

To which the Goncourt brothers added the postscript: "To all of this we raised no objection. But we have the feeling that when this time comes to science, God with His white beard will come down to earth, swinging a bunch of keys, and will say to humanity, the way they say at five o'clock at the salon: 'Closing time, gentlemen!'"

NEWS CHRONOLOGY

SEPTEMBER, 1950—AUGUST, 1951

SEPTEMBER, 1950

1ST. PRESIDENT TRUMAN tells nation, in a radio and television broadcast, that armed forces will expand from 1½ million to 3 million as we are "engaged once more in the age-old struggle for human liberty." He outlines U.S. "aims and hopes which he wants the world to understand."

A LETTER WRITTEN BY PRESIDENT TRUMAN sets off controversy after insertion in Congressional Record. In reply to request urging full Marine representation on Joint Chiefs of Staff, Mr. Truman remarked that the Marines "have a propaganda machine that is almost equal to Stalin's."

6TH. PRES. TRUMAN APOLOGIZES to Marines for his "unfortunate choice of language" in a letter to Marine Corps commandant.

8TH. DEFENSE PRODUCTION ACT is signed by President Truman as he appoints W. Stuart Symington to coordinate administration of the powers given the executive branch over the nations remobilization drive.

11TH. JAN CHRISTIAAN SMUTS 80, Field Marshall and Prime Minister of South Africa 1919-24, 1939-48, dies of a heart attack. Smuts was among the leading architects of the British Commonwealth of Nations, League of Nations and the UN.

12TH. GEN. OMAR BRADLEY, chairman of the Joint Cheifs of Staff, is unanimously approved by the Senate for the rank of a five-star general.

DEFENSE SECY. JOHNSON resigns, explaining that he "made more enemies than friends" since he replaced James Forrestal. Pres. Truman accepts his resignation and selects Gen. of the Army Marshall to succeed him.

15TH. UN TROOPS land at Inchon, a west coast port 18 miles from Seoul and 150 north of the main battlefront. Landing, directed by Gen. MacArthur, and spearheaded by elements of the Marine Corps, followed 2 days of the heaviest air-sea bombardment of the Korean war.

18TH. WILLIAM O'DWYER's appointment as Ambassador to Mexico is confirmed by Senate after heated debate, 42-22.

19TH. ATLANTIC FOREIGN MINISTERS serve notice on Russia and East Germany that they will fight to defend West Germany and Berlin.

20TH. INTERNAL SECURITY BILL requiring all Communists to register is passed by both houses of Congress.

SENATE CONFIRMS MARSHALL'S appointment as a new Defense Sec'y. by a vote of 57-11.

22ND. NOBEL PEACE PRIZE is awarded to Dr. Ralph Bunche, first Negro recipient, and 11th American so honored.

25TH. PAUL G. HOFFMAN resigns chairmanship of E.C.A., is replaced by W. C. Foster.

28TH. INDONESIA'S ADMISSION as 60th UN member is approved by the General Assembly, after initial approval of the Council.

29TH. GEN. MACARTHUR enters Seoul with South Korean President Syngman Rhee, restoring the city as the capital of Korea.

SECURITY COUNCIL votes 7-3 to invite Chinese Communists to appear at the UN, in order to discuss Formosan situation.

30TH. CONGRESSIONAL MEDAL OF HONOR is awarded by Pres. Truman to Maj. Gen. William Dean for "gallantry and intrepidity" in leading his troops against Taejon.

OCTOBER, 1950

1ST. SOUTH KOREAN troops cross 38th parallel as Reds ignor surrender plea issued by Gen. MacArthur.

PHILADELPHIA PHILLIES win first National League baseball pennant since 1915. N. Y. Yankees triumph in American League.

4TH. STOCK EXCHANGE prices rise to highest levels in four years.

UN GENERAL ASSEMBLY gives Gen. MacArthur tacit consent to launch all-out invasion of North Korea, as South Korean forces race due north above the 38th.

7TH. FIRST AMERICAN TROOPS cross 38th parallel as segments of the First Cavalry capture Kaesong.

TURKEY IS ELECTED to the Security Council of UN by a 53-4 vote of the General Assembly.

N. Y. YANKEES sweep four game World Series by beating Philadelphia 5-2, before 68,098 spectators at Yankee Stadium, N. Y.

11TH. COLUMBIA BROADCASTING SYSTEM wins F.C.C. permission to go ahead with its color television programs as rival companies plan court actions to combat ruling.

12TH. RUSSIA VETOES UN recommendation that Secy. Gen. Trygve Lie be reelected for a five-year term.

12TH. PRESIDENT TRUMAN flies to Pacific

for secret conferences with Gen. MacArthur.

14TH. COMPLETE UNANIMITY of views on the Korean situation is expressed by Pres. Truman and Gen. MacArthur at the conclusion of their five-hour conference on Wake Island. The President lauds MacArthur "as one of America's great soldier-statesmen."

19TH. SIR STAFFORD CRIPPS, 61, resigns as Chancellor of the Exchequer and member of Parliament.
UN DIVISIONS break through to Pyongyang, capital of North Korea.
EDNA ST. VINCENT MILLAY, 58, one of America's leading poets, dies at her home in Austerlitz, N. Y.
CONNIE MACK retires as field manager of the Philadelphia Athletics after managing the baseball club for 50 years.

20TH. HENRY LEWIS STIMSON, 83, State Secretary under Pres. Hoover and War Secretary under Presidents Taft, Roosevelt and Truman, dies in Huntington, N. Y. of a heart attack.

23RD. AL JOLSON, 67, stage, screen and radio singer dies in San Francisco.

24TH. CHINESE COMMUNISTS accept UN invitation to appear before the Security Council to air charges of alleged U.S. aggression in Formosa.

26TH. SOUTH KOREANS reach Manchurian frontier as North Korean armies muster their last resources.

27TH. CHINESE COMMUNIST troops enter Korean war without any notice or declaration of intervention. UN forces reel back under savage attacks by Chinese divisions.

29TH. KING GUSTAV V, 92, of Sweden dies after reigning nearly 43 years.

30TH. RED CHINA ARMY moves on Llasa, capital of Tibet, as 15 year-old Dalai Lama prepares to take flight.

NOVEMBER, 1950

1ST. PRESIDENT TRUMAN escapes assassination attempt made by 2 Puerto Rican Nationalists at the entrance to Blair House, the President's temporary residence. One assassin is killed, the other wounded. One guard is also slain, and two other police officers wounded.
TRYGVE LIE'S term as UN Secretary General is extended 3 years by a 46-5 vote of the General Assembly.

2ND. GEORGE BERNARD SHAW, 94, greatest playwright of his time, dies in England.
U.S. POPULATION now stands at 150,-697,361, according to figures released by the Census Bureau.

4TH. UN GEN. ASSEMBLY passes resolution taking Spain off the blacklist for full diplomatic relations with UN countries.

6TH. RED CHINA'S 11th hour intervention in Korea is scored by Gen. MacArthur in a note to the UN. MacArthur declared, "UN forces are meeting a new foe . . . are presently in contact with Chinese Communist military units."

7TH. REPUBLICANS MARK a series of unexpected gains in Senate, Congressional and gubernatorial elections, but fail to gain control of Congress.
VINCENT IMPELLITTERI, running as an independent, becomes first Mayor to defeat both major machines in New York City.

10TH. NOBEL PRIZES are awarded to William Faulkner and Bertrand Russell in literature, to C. F. Powell in physics and to Otto Diels and Kurt Adler in chemistry.

16TH. GRAND JURY INDICTS 34 persons, including Harry Gross, head of a $20 million gambling business on charges of bookmaking and criminal conspiracy.

17TH. 5-YEAR ECONOMIC aid for the Philippines, calling for a $250 million loan, is

announced by the ECA.

22ND. 77 KILLED, 300 INJURED in a Long Island R.R. train wreck in Richmond Hill, Queens, N. Y. C.

26TH. CHINESE REDS seize offensive along entire Korean front, driving back outnumbered UN forces. Many UN units face encirclement as Red divisions storm ahead.
ATOMIC ENERGY COMMISSION selects 250,000-acre site in South Carolina as a location for plants in which hydrogen bomb will be developed.

30TH. PRES. TRUMAN designates Mayor Michael V. DiSalle, 43, of Toledo, Ohio as Director of Price Stabilization.

DECEMBER, 1950

4TH. CHINESE OFFENSIVE makes great gains with Pyongyang, capital of North Korea, falling into their hands without a fight. TRUMAN AND ATLEE meet in Washington for a series of talks centering on the Chinese intervention in Korea.

5TH. CHARLES ROSS, 65, press secretary to Pres. Truman dies of a heart attack.

7TH. GEN. LATTRE DE TASSIGNY, 60, is appointed supreme civilian and military commander in Indo-China.
ALGER HISS' conviction is upheld by the U.S. Court of Appeals in New York.

8TH. PRIME MINISTER ATLEE visits UN after his 5-day stay in Washington, D. C. Appeals for an "effective organization if we want to preserve peace."
PRES. TRUMAN nominates Joseph Short, Jr., to succeed the late Charles Ross as White House press secretary.

11TH. NORTHEASTERN KOREA evacuated by 60,000 stranded UN troops, as main UN forces fall back to positions below 38th.

16TH. PRES. TRUMAN proclaims "the existence of a national emergency" warning that "our homes, our nation, are in great danger."

OFFICE OF DEFENSE MOBILIZATION is created by Pres. Truman with Charles E. Wilson as director.

18TH. NORTH ATLANTIC DEFENSE MINISTERS approve a master plan for integration of their land, air and sea forces and use of German brigades. Gen. Dwight Eisenhower is named supreme Atlantic commander, as the Ministers prepare to return home from their meeting in Brussels.

19TH. RED CHINA'S delegation to the UN leaves New York after rejecting all peace overtures.

23RD. LT. GEN. WALKER, 61, U.S. 8th Army commander is killed when his armored jeep crashes into a supply truck near Seoul.
LT. GEN. M. B. RIDGWAY, 55, is named successor to Gen. Walker.

27TH. STANTON GRIFFIS is named Ambassador to Spain by Pres. Truman.

JANUARY, 1951

1ST. CHINESE-KOREAN RED drive for Seoul begins as UN forces are hurled back from positions near 38th parallel.

4TH. REDS TAKE Seoul, Kimpo Airfield and the port of Inchon, as U.S. 8th Army continues retreat.

5TH. SENATOR TAFT opens congressional foreign policy debate by accusing the President of sending troops to Korea without consent of Congress.

8TH. PRES. TRUMAN delivers State of Union message warning Congress that "the Soviet rulers may face the facts and lay aside their plans to take over the world."

10TH. SINCLAIR LEWIS, 65, America's famed novelist, dies in Rome of a heart ailment.

17TH. BURMESE COURT finds Dr. Gordon Seagrave, legendary "Burma Surgeon," guilty of high treason and sentences him to 6 years imprisonment.
PRES. TRUMAN receives credentials of Spanish Ambassador Jose Lequerica, ending a 5-year suspension of U.S.-Spanish diplomatic relations.

19TH. ERIC JOHNSTON is appointed new Economic Stabilization Administrator by Pres. Truman, replacing Alan Valentine.

27TH. ATOMIC EXPLOSION, first in a series of new tests, is set off by Government at testing grounds in New Mexico.
FIELD MARSHALL GUSTAV MANNERHEIM, 83, President of Finland 1944-1946, national soldier-statesman, dies in Switzerland.

30TH. UN PASSES RESOLUTION branding Red China as aggressor, after two weeks of bitter debate.

31ST. GETULIO VARGAS, 67, is inaugurated President of Brazil in lavish ceremonies marking his return to power.

FEBRUARY, 1951

1ST. GEN. DWIGHT EISENHOWER reports to Congress on his European survey emphasizing the "rejuvenation" of the "spirit to resist," a feeling that can be intensified by greater American military aid.

6TH. WORST U.S. RAIL DISASTER in 33 years kills 83 persons, injures 500, when Pennsylvania Railroad commuters' train plunges from tracks as it starts over a temporary overpass at Woodbridge, N. J. Seven separate investigations launched by officials.
NATIONWIDE RAILROAD strike begins to crack as some of 120,000 idle workers start returning to key stations.

7TH. WILLIAM REMMINGTON, 33, former Commerce Dept. economist is found guilty of perjury. He had denied membership in the Communist party, and proclaimed complete innocence as to espionage.

9TH. HOOVER, calling his radio talk, "the speech of my life," expands his views
(Continued on Page 396)

PHOTO DATA
——— *International Section* ———

RYUICHI AMANO, *Japan*: page 207. *Photo data*: photograph made by the pendulum light-pattern method.

STEN DIDRIK BELLANDER, *Sweden*: page 172. (Photo data not available.)

BERINGER & PAMPALUCHI, *Switzerland*: page 224. *Photo data*: camera Makina: aperture f/9: exposure 1/100th second.

WERNER BISCHOF, *Switzerland*: page 237. (Photo data not available.)

EMIL BRUNNER, *Switzerland*: pages 238-239, 240, 241. (See pages 238-241.)

BOHUSLAV BURIAN, *Czechoslovakia*: page 182. *Photo data*: camera Rolleiflex: lens Tessar: film Foma: aperture f/8: exposure 1/50th second.

HENRI CARTIER-BRESSON, *France*: page 236. (Photo data not available.)

GEORGE CSERNA, *Switzerland*: pages 161-170. (See pages 161-162.)

ADALBERT DEFNER, *Austria*: page 177. Defner is one of the best known pictorial photographers of the Tyrol in Austria. (Photo data not available.)

ROBERT DOISNEAU, *France*: page 189. *Photo data*: camera Rolleiflex: lens Tessar: film Super XX: aperture f/5.6: exposure 1/100th second.

BERTIL FORSEN, *Sweden*: page 173. *Photo data*: Made on assignment for the newspaper *Expressen*. Portrays a soccer goalie leaping in anger after missing the ball.

ANGEL GARMENDIA, *Mexico*: pages 200-201. *Photo data*: camera Rolleiflex: lens Tessar: aperture f/8: exposure 1/100th second.

JULES GEIGER, *France*: page 188. *Photo data*: camera Rolleiflex: lens Tessar: aperture f/5.6 film Isochrome fine grain: exposure 1/50th second.

ARMIN HAAB, *Switzerland*: pages 216-217. *Photo data*: camera Rolleiflex: lens Tessar: aperture f/5.6: film Super XX: exposure 1/300th second.

GUSTAV HANSSON, *Sweden*: pages 180, 181. *Photo data*: (page 180) camera Rolleiflex: lens Tessar: film Ansco Supreme: aperture f/11: exposure 1/100th second; (page 181) camera Rolleiflex: lens Tessar: film Ilford: aperture f/8: exposure 1/50th second.

E. A. HEINIGER, *Switzerland*: page 221. *Photo data*: (*top photo*) The Alletsch Glacier: camera Linhof: lens Dagor: film Panatomic X: aperture f/12: exposure 1/50th second; (*bottom photo*) The Matterhorn: camera Linhof: lens Dagor: aperture f/18: exposure 5 seconds with a red filter.

FRANK HURLEY, *Australia*: pages 226-231. *Photo data*: (pages 226-227) camera Graflex: lens Tessar: film Super XX: aperture f/8: exposure made at 1/50th second with an Aero II filter; (pages 228-229) camera 5x7 view: lens Cooke: film Tri-X Kodak: aperture f/11: exposure made at 1/50th second with 23A filter; (page 230) camera Linhof: lens Tessar: film Super XX: aperture f/11: exposure 1/50th second; (page 231) camera 6x8 field view: lens Tessar: film Super XX: aperture f/11: exposure 1/50th second.

IZIS, *France*: page 178. *Photo data*: camera Rolleiflex: lens Tessar: film Plus X: aperture f/11: exposure 1/50th second.

PETER KEETMAN, *Germany*: page 225. *Photo data*: Pictures made by the pendulum light-pattern method.

AART KLEIN, *Holland*: pages 202, 203. *Photo data*: (page 202) camera Rolleiflex: lens Tessar: film Super XX: aperture f/5.6: exposure 1/100th second; (page 203) camera Rolleiflex: lens Tessar: film Super XX: aperture f/5.6: exposure 1/250th second.

MAX KOLB, *Switzerland*: page 171. (Photo data not available.)

OSKAR KREISEL, *Germany*: page 225. *Photo data*: camera Leica: lens Hektor: film Super XX: aperture f/11: exposures of water droplets made with electronic multi-flash.

ROY KUROKAWA, *Japan*: pages 212-213. *Photo data*: camera Speed Graphic: lens Wollensak: aperture f/8: film Ansco Supreme: exposure made with a stroboscopic flash unit.

MAX KUTTEL, *Germany*: pages 218, 219. *Photo data*: (page 218) camera Rolleiflex: lens Tessar: film Super XX: aperture f/8: exposure 1/50th second; (page 219) camera Rolleiflex: lens Tessar: film Super XX: aperture f/5.6: exposure 1/50th second.

ERGY LANDAU, *France*: page 179. (Photo data not available.)

SIEGFRIED LAUTERWASSER, *Germany*: pages 192, 193. Lauterwasser took these pictures during elections in Switzerland. *Photo data*: (page 192) camera Contax: lens Sonnar: film Super XX: exposure by meter for each picture; (page 193) camera Contax: lens Sonnar: film Super XX: aperture f/8: exposure 1/100th second.

JEAN MANZON, *France*: pages 184-185, 205, 222, 223. *Photo data*: (pages 184-185) camera Rolleiflex: lens Tessar: film Super XX: aperture f/8: exposure 1/100th second with two flash bulbs; (page 205) camera Rolleiflex: lens Tessar: film Super XX: aperture f/11: exposure 1/10 second with two flash bulbs; (page 222) camera Rolleiflex: lens Tessar: film Super XX: aperture f/3.5: exposure 1/5th second; (page 223)

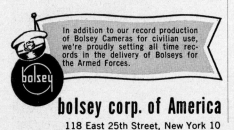
camera Speed Graphic: lens Kodak: film Super XX: aperture f/11: exposure 1/50th second with yellow filter.

ADOLF MORATH, *England*: page 220, 235. *Photo data*: camera Rolleiflex: lens Tessar with Proxar attachment: film Panatomic X: aperture f/22: exposure 1/2 second with two 500-watt photofloods.

ATSUSHI NAKAFUJI, *Japan*: page 209. (Photo data not available.)

PAUL & JEAN PICHONNIER, *Belgium*: pages 186, 187. (Photo data not available.)

AXEL POIGNANT, *Australia*: page 194. *Photo data*: camera Rolleiflex: lens Tessar: aperture f/8: exposure 1/100th second.

GEORGES RADO, *Brazil*: page 234. (Photo data not available.)

WOLFGANG REISEWITZ, *Germany*: page 17. (Photo data not available.)

REGINA RELANG, *Germany*: page 204. *Photo data*: camera Rolleiflex: lens Tessar: aperture f/3.5: exposure 1/10 second.

JACQUES ROUCHON, *France*: page 190. *Photo data*: camera Contax: lens Sonnar: film Super XX: aperture f/4: exposure 1/50th second.

SAVITRY, *France*: page 191. *Photo data*: camera Rolleiflex: lens Tessar: film Super XX: exposure 1/50th second with floodlights.

SERGE DE SAZO, *France*: pages 196, 197. (See page 196.)

GEORGE SCHMIDT, *Germany*: page 195. *Photo data*: All studies made with a Leica 3C equipped with an Elmar lens and close-up attachments. Time exposures used with natural light.

BRUNO STEFANI, *Italy*: page 206. *Photo data*: camera Leica: lens Elmar: film Panatomic X: aperture f/6.3: exposure 1/100th second.

ALBERT STEINER, *Switzerland*: pages 174, 175. *Photo data*: (page 174) camera Reise: lens Optik: aperture f/6: exposure 1/100th second; (page 175) camera Reise: lens Optik: aperture f/32: exposure 1/25th second.

W. SUSCHITZKY, *England*: pages 148, 198, 199. *Photo data*: (page 198) camera Rolleiflex: lens Tessar: aperture f/11: exposure 1/100th second; (page 199) camera Rolleiflex: lens Tessar: aperture f/16: exposure 1/50th second with yellow filter.

GEORGES VIOLLON, *France*: page 183. (Photo data not available.)

JUN YOSHIDA, *Japan*: page 208. *Photo data*: camera Rolleiflex: lens Tessar: film Sakura: aperture f/8: exposure 1/100th second with one flash bulb.

SENZO YOSHIOKA, *Japan*: pages 210, 211, 214-215. *Photo data*: (page 210) camera Leica: lens Elmar: aperture f/5.6: exposure 1/60th second; (page 211) camera Speed Graphic: lens Ektar: film Super XX: aperture f/11: exposure 1/50th second with one flash bulb; (pages 214-215) camera Speed Graphic: lens Ektar: film Ansco: aperture f/8: exposure 1 second.

NEWS CHRONOLOGY

(Continued from Page 394)

on making an "American Gibraltar" as an alternative to pouring men and arms into Europe and Asia.

11TH. GOV. DEWEY assails Hoover's isolationist views saying it would be "suicide" for U.S. to withdraw to Western Hemisphere defenses.

14TH. RAY ROBINSON becomes first welterweight boxer in history to dethrone a middleweight champion, when he defeats Jake LaMotta in the 13th round of their bout in New York.

15TH. GREAT BRITAIN nationalizes its entire iron and steel production, despite fierce opposition of Conservative party.

18TH. CHINESE COMMUNIST offensive fails along entire front as UN troops seize initiative, advancing towards Seoul.

19TH. ANDRE GIDE, 81, French writer, winner of Nobel Prize for literature, dies in Paris.

26TH. CONSTITUTIONAL AMENDMENT barring election of a President for more than 2 terms is ratified as Nevada becomes the 36th state to sign.

28TH. SENATE CRIME INVESTIGATING committee releases report stating that 2 major crime syndicates operate and control U.S. underworld activity.

MARCH, 1951

5TH. PARIS HOST to meeting of Big 4 Deputy Foreign Ministers, who convene in attempt to settle previously stalemated issues.

CRIMINAL PROCEEDINGS against Dr. A. G. Paz, publisher of La Prensa, are ordered as pro-Peron police shut down the newspaper's facilities.

7TH. IRANIAN PREMIER, Gen. Ali Razmara, long a friend of Western oil interests, is assassinated by a religious fanatic.

OSCAR COLLAZO, survivor of 2 Puerto Rican Nationalists who tried to assassinate Pres. Truman, is convicted of first-degree murder.

12TH. ALGER HISS faces immediate imprisonment as Supreme Court refuses to review his perjury conviction.

14TH. SEOUL REOCCUPIED by UN forces driving due north towards the 38th parallel.

15TH. FRANK COSTELLO, notorious underworld figure, walks out on hearing of Senate Crime Investigating Committee in New York as record-sized TV audience watches proceedings.

17TH. IRANIAN SENATE votes for oil nationalization despite vigorous British protests.

19TH. SCHUMAN PLAN calling for eliminating of trade restrictions in coal and steel, is approved by delegates of France, Belgium, West Germany, Italy, Netherlands and Luxembourg.

21ST. WILLIAM O'DWYER's name is linked to suspected underworld ties as Senate Crime committee winds up New York hearings.

22ND. ALGER HISS surrenders to federal officials to begin his 5-year perjury sentence.

24TH. GEN. MACARTHUR's truce bid to commander of Red Chinese forces is scored by State Department and Defense Chiefs who claim that all peace feelers must be initially passed on by Washington.

28TH. FRENCH PRESIDENT Vincent Auriol arrives in New York marking first formal visit ever paid to U.S. by a president of the Republic of France.

APRIL, 1951

4TH. U.S. SENATE votes 69-21 to transfer 4 divisions to Europe for service under Gen. Eisenhower.

5TH. ATOMIC SPIES, Julius Rosenberg and his wife, Ethel, are sentenced to death after being convicted of transmitting U.S. secrets to Russia. Co-conspirator, Morton Sobell, is given 30 year imprisonment term.

11TH. GEN. MACARTHUR, is dismissed by Pres. Truman from his 4 UN, Allied and U.S. commands in the Far East.

LT. GEN. MATTHEW RIDGWAY is named to replace Gen. MacArthur.

14TH. ERNEST BEVIN, 70, former Foreign Minister, dies in London of a heart attack.

18TH. SEN. ARTHUR VANDENBURG, 67, GOP policy leader, champion of international cooperation, dies in Grand Rapids, Michigan, from aggravated lung and spine conditions.

19TH. GEN. MACARTHUR, speaking with "neither rancor nor bitterness" addresses a joint session of Congress, declaring that the U.S. Chiefs of Staff shared his views on "military" actions in Korea.

20TH. NEW YORK CITY gives Gen. Mac-
Arthur and his family biggest and noisiest
welcome in the city's history as an estimated 7,500,000 people mob the streets.
22ND. 400,000 COMMUNISTS launch suicidal
attacks along entire Korean front, driving
UN forces south of the 38th parallel.
LABOR MINISTER BEVAN of great Britain
quits his office after months of strife within
the party over sacrificing socialist program
to concentrate on rearmament.
23RD. CHARLES DAWES, 85, U.S. Vice President under Coolidge, dies in Chicago.
28TH. ROBERT VOGELER, 39, vice-president
of the Intl. Telephone & Telegraph Corp.
is released by Hungary after 17 months
imprisonment as a U.S. spy.

MAY, 1951

7TH. DEFENSE SEC'Y. MARSHALL appears
before Congressional committee answering
MacArthur's claims asserting that present
U.S. tactics can "develop the best probabil-
ities for reaching a satisfactory negotiatory
basis."
11TH. JAMES J. MORAN, ex-N.Y.C. Water
Commissioner and close friend of ex-Mayor
O'Dwyer, is sentenced to 5 years in jail
after being found guilty of perjury.
21ST. FAIR TRADE LAWS CURBED by a ruling
of the Supreme Court to the effect that re-
tailers who refuse to sign pricing agreements are not liable to state "fair trade"
laws.
24TH. MAJOR COMMUNIST Spring offensive
flounders as UN forces inflict enormous
casualties on the attackers.
25TH. GEN. COLLINS, Army Chief of Staff,
tells Congress that MacArthur sent American troops to the Manchurian frontier in
violation of a "clearcut directive" to let
only South Koreans go to the border.
SUCCESSFUL COMPLETION of H-bomb tests
on Eniwetok Atoll is reported by the
A.E.C. and the Defense Dept.
29TH. DEPARTMENT STORES in New York
start a price cutting war following Supreme
Court's decision against state "fair-trade"
laws. Hordes of shoppers storm price-cut-
ting stores.
FANNY BRICE, 59, creator of Baby Snooks,
veteran Ziegfeld Follies star, dies in Hollywood.

JUNE, 1951

1ST. DEAN ACHESON denies Red appease-
ment as he appears before Senate Foreign
Relations Committee. Upholds ouster of
MacArthur.
4TH. DR. SERGE KOUSSEVITZKY, conductor-
emeritus of Boston Symphony Orchestra,
dies in Boston.
SUPREME COURT, by a 6-2 decision upholds
conviction of 11 U.S. Communist leaders.
7TH. BRITAIN reveals that an international
search is under way for 2 missing Forgn.
Office officials well posted on inter-Allied
secrets. The 2 who vanished are Donald
MacLean, and Guy Burgess, both noted
for left-wing sympathies.
11TH. SENATE PASSES BILL to send aid to
India in the form of a $190 million loan.
The loan will facilitate the purchase of
much needed grain and other basic food
supplies.
13TH. NATIONS' ATOMIC EXPERTS report that
the April-May atomic tests at Eniwetok
Atoll "contributed to the eventual development" of the hydrogen bomb.
EAMON DE VALERA, 68, former Irish Prime
Minister is returned to office 74-69 over
incumbent John Costello.
20TH. 21 LEADING COMMUNISTS arrested by
F.B.I. in New York. Hours later a grand

397

jury indicts them for violation of the Smith Act.

23RD. JACOB MALIK, Soviet UN representative, voices a Korean truce plea asserting that "there is a sincere desire to put an end to the bloody fighting in Korea."

25TH. PRESIDENT TRUMAN ANSWERS MALIK by declaring that "we are ready to join in a peaceful settlement in Korea", adding "it must be a real settlement which fully ends the aggression and restores peace." MACARTHUR HEARINGS end before Senate committee after 42 days and 2,045,000 words of testimony.

30TH. GENERAL RIDGWAY broadcasts a proposal to the Reds in Korea calling for a military cease-fire.

JULY, 1951

1ST. RED PEKING RADIO broadcasts counter-proposal to UN commander Ridgway stating that the North Korean and Chinese communists agree to a 'peace' meeting to be held at Kaesong between July 10-15.

2ND. 4 TOP COMMUNIST PARTY LEADERS jump bail as seven surrender.

3RD. GEN. RIDGWAY broadcasts his acceptance for a field peace parley.

4TH. WILLIAM N. OATIS, 37, Associated Press correspondent in Prague, is sentenced to ten years imprisonment on charges of espionage.

5TH. THE UN AND KOREAN REDS agree to begin cease-fire negotiations in the field on July 8; the initial meetings to be held in the 'neutral' city of Kaesong.

8TH. UN AND RED LIAISON TEAMS complete arrangements for the truce conference to be held at Kaesong on July 10.

10TH. TRUCE DELEGATIONS led by Admiral Joy and General Nam meet for the first time in Kaesong to organize an agenda for cease-fire negotiations.

12TH. DRAFT OF A JAPANESE PEACE TREATY is published by England and the U.S.; as a preliminary move to an international peace conference to be held in San Francisco on September 3.

16TH. ADMIRAL FORREST SHERMAN confers with Franco on a possible U.S.-Spanish defense agreement.

17TH. LEOPOLD III, 49, ABDICATES after 17 years as King of the Belgians and is succeeded by his son, Baudouin I.

18TH. WORST FLOODS on record in the Kansas City area take over 40 lives, and cause an estimated $750 million-$1 billion damage.

19TH. FRANCO REVAMPS CABINET with pro-Western officials appointed in an effort to offset criticism of his government.

20TH. KING ABDULLAH IBN HUSSIEN, 69, of Jordan is assassinated in Jerusalem.

22ND. ADMIRAL FORREST SHERMAN, 54, U.S. Chief of Naval Operations dies in Naples after two heart attacks. He had visited Madrid, Paris and London to discuss Western defense plans.

23RD. MARSHAL PETAIN, 95, dies in his prison-villa on the Island of Yeu, off the French mainland.

27TH. FEDERAL NARCOTICS AND SECRET SERVICE agents in New York trap 12 alleged members of a $30 million French-Italian narcotics and counterfeit money ring believed headed by Lucky Luciano.

30TH. FREDERICK VANDERBILT FIELDS and Abner Green, Civil Rights Bail Fund trustees already jailed for contempt of court, are given additional 6-month contempt sentences in New York.

31ST. 12 CALIFORNIA COMMUNISTS leaders are seized by the FBI and indicted by a federal grand jury in Los Angeles.

DAN ABEL KIMBALL is sworn in to succeed Francis P. Matthews as Secy. of the Navy.

U. S. CAMERA · 1952

(Continued from Page 8)

Town. And we're particularly fortunate that the photographer himself is so fond of the series of pictures that he wrote a special text to accompany them.

The ageless magic of Edward Steichen's photography of the theater is represented on page 136 in his powerful study of the march of Moses and the Isrealites to the Promised Land in *The Green Pastures,* which was revived on Broadway last spring. Steichen made the photo for *Vanity Fair* in which it appeared in May 1930.

The Audubon section is a tribute to one of photography's unsung achievements. The work of Allan Cruickshank and the Audubon editors who select the random pictures that make the Society's files a mine as golden as the throats of the birds depicted, is a solid and special one.

It seems as though there is a special Elisofon niche in every issue of U. S. Camera Annual. Well, there is always Elisofon—with always a new and infectious idea. If this is the net series of pictures to end all such series, it is also the nicest netting of nets we've ever netted. So it's net to everyone—reader—editor—Elisofon.

Scattered all through the Annual are pictures taken by the White House Press Photographers. Their work encompasses far more than the White House and the Washington scene. This year's show of their work was so outstanding, 19 pages of it is an important part of the Annual.

There are so many good individual pictures it would be foolish to single out any here. There are many new names—as always, and, not so many of the old. This is U. S. Camera's desire to be current. This is a yearbook of photography's work of the year. So names change—rapidly. It is a pity, however, that many of the older, well-recognized photographers are so occupied with the wholesome task of making a living that our best efforts and their best promises don't get together in a picture or two for U. S. Camera's pages.

The saddest part of the photo year was the death of Robert Flaherty. He had become a benign symbol of the phase of photography that wasn't his invention but certainly his domain—the documentary. A movie producer for most of his life, his *Nanook, Man of Aran, Louisiana Story* and *White Shadows* were the core of an interpretive nature that delineated man, his problems and his struggle for survival as it hasn't been done before—or since. This is a name as great to the films as David Wark Griffith's. To still photography his contribution was also great. It was Flaherty's influence that engendered the best in present day documentary work.

Once again U. S. Camera thanks the many persons and agencies whose cooperation and assistance have made this Annual possible. In addition to the three editorial assistants the following have been of great service: Ed Hannigan, who did the Photo article in the Mobilization Section; Jonathan Tichenor, William Cannon and Terry Maloney who assisted with the captions; Phil Brody who did the production; Doug McIntosh and Hugh Mulvena who handled business details and Elsie DeMary the distribution: also John H. Waddell of *Wollensak Optical Co.* who assisted in obtaining pictures for the Photo article in Mobilization.

Thanks also go to the magazines, news services and photo agencies which have made so many photographs available to U. S. Camera, among which are: *Life, Black Star, Magnum, Rapho-Guillumette, International News Photos, Wide World* and *Acme.*

—TOM MALONEY

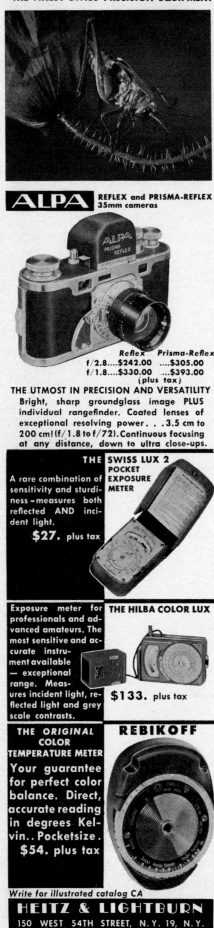
AUDUBON
(Continued from Page 113)

Komorowski is a film editor for *Fox* films; Hal Harrison writes a nature column for the *Pittsburgh Gazette*; Samuel Grimes runs an engraving plant in Jacksonville, Fla.

Several hundreds of the photographs are individual shots sent to the Society by amateurs interested in birds or lucky enough to have taken an unusual bird picture. Allan Cruickshank is a soft-spoken individual who must be one of the most patient men in the picture-taking field. Some of his work has taken months of preparation for a single shot. His working conditions, especially in the Florida Everglades are more than rugged. And each year—he's been the Society's photographer for 16 years—he arrives in New York with more of the fine photos that make Audubon and Cruickshank synonymous.

The pictures shown on these seven pages have not been culled carefully from the generous files at Audubon headquarters. They are a random group chosen mainly from pictures that haven't been used in U.S. Camera in the past. They show what photo quality is—what satisfactory professional results can be achieved by hobbyists—including Cruickshank who has made himself the fortunate possessor of a profession based on the life and pursuit he loves. They also show what competence and enthusiasm can do with a camera. This is sound fine work with no flourishes or frills. This is the kind of picture-taking that makes almost every viewer feel that he too could do these photos—if he had the time and opportunity. Of course he could and every once in a while he does. Pictures like these have made the *National Geographic Magazine* one of the greatest, and the Audubon Society the respected and loved force in wild life conservation that it is.

Founded in 1905, the National Audubon Society is the oldest and largest national conservation organization in North America. Its annual budget of about $500,000 is entirely privately financed through membership dues, contributions and bequests.

With the exception of the photos of the mother robin feeding her young *(upper right, page 114)* photographed by G. T. Hillman, and of the pelicans *(page 114)* made by George Komorowski, all of the photographs in this section were taken by Allan Cruickshank.